Theory of the firm

Modern economics
Series editor: David W Pearce

Theory of the firm

Michael A Crew

Longman
LONDON and NEW YORK

Longman Group Limited
Burnt Mill
Harlow
Essex CM20 2JE

Distributed in the United States of America by
Longman Inc., New York

Associated companies, branches and representatives throughout the world

© M. A. Crew, 1975

First published, 1975

ISBN 0 582 44043 2 Paper
ISBN 0 582 44042 4 Cased

Library of Congress Catalog Card Number: 74—83136

Printed in Great Britain by
Whitstable Litho Ltd

Contents

Preface

If, as Cliff Lloyd has argued, "to write a textbook is to publicly admit to the sins of vanity, greed and incompetence. . . ." (Lloyd, 1967, p. ix) (References are on p. 165), then every economist embarking upon such a task should examine his motives very carefully. In this case there is the justification that relatively few textbooks have yet appeared on the theory of the firm. This, and the fact that it is a rapidly developing area, does partially enable almost any author in the field to attempt to display some originality, and hence avoid Lloyd's charge of incompetence. This book does offer some original features. It attempts to show some of the relationships between the theory of the firm and public policy, and scope for possible developments in this area. It also attempts to indicate the extent to which the theory is a developing field by criticizing existing work and by indicating scope for future developments. In other respects, except possibly for the rather detailed exercises and worked answers to many of these, the book covers ground common to other textbooks. It makes no claim to novelty on some aspects of the exposition of the theory. For the most part, however, the exposition is, hopefully, different in at least some respects from existing texts.

A note on the exercises is in order. Most chapters contain numerical or even mathematical examples. These are meant to serve three purposes:

1.   To enable the reader to check that he understands certain prerequisites, e.g., any concepts borrowed from demand theory.

2.   To enable the reader to check his understanding of the chapter.

3.   To extend the material developed in the chapter.

Most of the exercises are in category (2). Experience in both learning and teaching has shown the benefit of solving numerical problems in developing confidence and understanding of the subject. Students and teachers are encouraged to use the examples fully. In most cases this will mean resisting the temptation immediately to turn to the "Solutions and hints" in the back of the book. In fact most students will find it helpful first to make a sustained attempt at solving the problem. If this does not work then they should turn to the text and find where this topic is dealt with. If this still does not work then they should turn to the "Solutions and hints". Finally, if this still does not help they will need to approach their teacher. Of course, not all readers will be interested in the exercises. Some readers, e.g., managers, civil servants, and the like, will only want to get a general view of the book, in which case they will not benefit from detailed study of the exercises.

The book does aim to be of some interest to non-specialists although some basic knowledge of elementary economics, intermediate demand theory, and elementary mathematics will prove useful. A fair amount of mathematical symbolism is employed. This should not be of concern to readers because, in fact, the derivation of mathematical results aims to be rather detailed and even pedestrian by the standard of many textbooks in economics. Thus the reader will find most of the steps between results derived for him, usually in the "Notes" which are identified in the text and found at the end of each chapter.

Acknowledgements

I am indebted to the following for permission to reproduce copyright material:

Addison-Wesley Publishing Company Inc. for an extract and symbols modified from pp. 72—3 of *Non Linear and Dynamic Programming* by G. Hadley; American Economic Association for an extract from "Theories of the Firm: Marginalist, Behavioral, Managerial" by F. Machlup from *American Economic Review*, No. 57, March 1967; and for Fig. 5.5 from *American Economic Review*, No. 61, March 1971; J. W. Arrowsmith Ltd for an extract from "Annual Survey of Economic Theory: The Theory of Monopoly" by J. R. Hicks from *Econometrica*, 3, 1, February 1935; Encyclopaedia Britannica Inc. for an extract from "The Nature and Causes of the Wealth of Nations" by Adam Smith from Encylopaedia Britannica, 1952; the editor of The Quarterly Journal of Economics and Harvard University Press for extracts from "Profits, Learning and the Convergence of Satisficing to Marginalism" by R. H. Day from *Quarterly Journal of Economics*, No. 81, May 1967; The Editor of Quarterly Review of Economics and Business for an extract from "The Break-up of the Maximization Principle" by G. L. Nordquist from *The Quarterly Review of Economics and Business*, 5, 3, Fall 1965; The Editor of Economica and The London School of Economics and Political Science for an extract from "Allocative Efficiency, X-Efficiency and the Measurement of Welfare Losses" by W. S. Comanor and H. Leibenstein from *Economica*, 36, August 1969, and The University of Chicago Press for an extract from "How to Cooperate in Business without really trying: A Learning Model of Decentralized Decision Making" by R. H. Day and Tinney from *Journal of Political Economy*, 26 July 1968.

I would like to acknowledge the help and interest of a number of people. I would like to thank E. Anthony Lowe for encouraging my interest in the theory of the firm while we were colleagues at the University of Bradford. I would like to acknowledge the help of William W. Cooper in demonstrating to me the importance of management science in the theory of the firm. Many of my ideas on the theory of the firm were developed as a result of a very fruitful period of collaboration in 1969–70 with Charles Rowley while we were colleagues at the University of Kent, and I would like to thank him for permission to utilize our earlier published work. Similarly, I would like to thank Paul Kleindorfer, and Michael Jones-Lee for permission to utilize our published work. I should also express my debt to the many students at the University of Bradford, Carnegie-Mellon University, University of Kent, University of Southampton, and Paisley College of Technology whose insistence on receiving clear exposition has helped me to clarify my own understanding of the subject. I am most grateful to Alistair Young, my colleague at Paisley, who read the entire manuscript with great care, and not only prevented me from making a number of mistakes but also given me the benefit of some of his insights on microeconomics. Not least in this list is David Pearce, the editor of the series to which this book belongs. His comments on the manuscript were very helpful indeed. In addition as a colleague and co-teacher of a microeconomic theory course at the University of Southampton, he was very helpful to me in developing the idea for this book and in conveying some of his own insights on teaching microeconomics and the theory of the firm.

I would like to acknowledge the benefit of valuable discussion with various people on detailed aspects of the work, especially Peter Simmons and Oliver Williamson. With such an impressive list as this the reader could be forgiven if he assumed that the book would be completely without error. Unfortunately errors of my own remain for which I alone am responsible.

I should like to acknowledge the expert typing assistance provided by my secretary, Jean Harris, whose patience at reading my, at times, almost illegible writing has taken on almost biblical proportions.

Finally, I should mention the understanding displayed by my wife, Hilary, who has now got used to my spending most evenings working on this book.

1

Introduction to the firm

The concern of economics with the behaviour of economic decision making has led it to develop models of the individual decision making units within the economy. The consumer and the firm are the two principal types of such units, apart from the government sector. The literature of economics has therefore developed theories of the consumer and of the firm. This book is concerned with the latter. The theory of the firm consists of a number of models most of which are very elegant and intellectually challenging. However, it is contended in this book that the theory of the firm should be studied for other reasons apart from the fact that it is (originally) an interesting area for academic study. Thus this chapter aims at answering a number of questions. Section 1.1 deals with the question: "What is the difference between the theory of the firm and real world firms?" Section 1.2 aims to answer the question: "What implications might the theory of the firm have for problems of firm and public policy?" Finally, by way of introduction to the topics covered and to the approach adopted in this book, section 1.3 is concerned with a brief historical survey of the controversies surrounding the theory of the firm in economics.

1.1 Firms and the theory of the firm

Every reader of this book knows what a firm is. He meets firms in his everyday life. Firms come in almost every shape and size. There are giant international firms like ICI, General Motors, Ford, Dupont, Shell, Esso, and Unilever. Their activities are considerable, extending over many products and many countries. At the other extreme there is the corner shop selling groceries, newspapers, or sweets. In contrast to the international corporations, the latter are often one-man businesses. The one man does everything himself, only buying in, on an occasional basis, the specialist services of an accountant or lawyer. The theory of the firm could attempt the apparently impossible task of producing a meaningful theory which in some sense is related to the vast range of organizations referred to as firms, from the corner shop to Esso[1]. Alternatively, different theories might be developed to suit different market structures.

At first sight the neoclassical theory of the firm seems to ignore the nature of firms entirely. The firm is regarded as a primitive concept, a device in an economically decentralized system for transforming input into output. Neoclassical theory seems to contribute nothing to reconciling the nature of, say, the complex conglomerate on the one hand with the sole trader on the other. Its simplicity, and its assumption of profit maximization, might make it seem closer to the sole trader than to the conglomerate. However, its ability to provide useful insights into industry, price, and even firm behaviour makes it of some relevance to not only small firms but also large complex firms. Thus the theory of the firm in perfect competition provides useful predictions concerning the response of prices, firms, and industries, for example, to changes in taxation or minimum-wage legislation; the theory of oligopoly reveals some of the complex inter-relations between firms which take place where there exists a few sellers of a product, a situation in which large firms often find themselves. However, while the neoclassical theory of the firm explores market relationships, and other relationships between firms, it bears little or no direct relevance to the internal organization of firms. This has not prevented the emergence of economic theories relating to the internal organization of firms.

Originating from the neoclassical theory of the firm is the work of Coase (1952), and Alchian and Demsetz (1972). Both are concerned with the nature of internal organization of firms and the role of the theory of the firm. Coase's contribution is to note that the firm, like the price mechanism, is essentially a coordinating device, a device which allocates resources within itself[2]. Coase points out that while the firm is concerned with allocating resources, unlike the price mechanism it does not have market and exchange transactions. As Coase says, "If a workman moves from department Y to department X, he does not go because of a change in relative prices, but because he is ordered to do so."[3] Coase's paper is concerned mainly with answering the question of why another co-ordinating device, in addition to the price mechanism, should exist. In short, he is concerned with the questions of why the firm is needed, and why this "supersession of the price mechanism" takes place. His answer is that "The main reason why it is profitable to establish a firm would seem to be that there is a cost of using the price mechanism" (Coase, 1952,

p. 336). The main cost of using the price mechanism is the cost of negotiating and concluding a separate contract for each transaction. The firm, on the other hand, greatly reduces the number of contracts that take place by performing functions internally instead of using the market. Thus the firm, instead of executing a series of contracts in the market to provide the activities performed by an employee, makes one contract (of employment) with the employee[4].

Another and related reason for the existence of the firm is that it may be desired to make a long-term contract to supply goods, in which case the costs of making one contract within the firm, rather than several shorter ones within the market, are lower. Risk also may make people want to enter long-term contracts, in which case it may be less costly if a firm undertakes the risk and, say, agrees to supply goods over a period, rather than conduct a number of transactions through the market some of which would be insurance services. It should be emphasized that the market puts an upper limit on the firm's costs. Thus the firm has to transact its activities at a lower cost than the market because it is always possible to revert to the market if it fails to do this. In summary then, the firm exists only because it can organize services "internally" which would otherwise cost more if channelled through markets.

Coase's theory is also relevant to the question of firm size and growth. In similar style is the recent contribution by Alchian and Demsetz, who extend the scope of Coase's work. They succeed in doing this principally by the introduction of two concepts which they call "team production" and "metering"[5]. Team production takes place where:

1. several types of resources are used;

2. the product is not the sum of separable outputs of each resource used by the team; and

3. not all the resources used by the team belong to one person (which creates what Alchian and Demsetz call the "team organizational problem").

These features of team production create a metering problem, that is, a measurement and apportionment problem. Problems of an economic organization include the metering of input productivity and the metering of rewards. Thus if rewards were random and not associated with productive effort then there would be no incentive toward productive effort. If rewards were negatively correlated with productivity then the organization would be subject to sabotage[6].

Sometimes the metering problem can be resolved by means of exchange in competitive markets where the market rewards those responsible for changes in output. The classic relationships in economics running from marginal productivity to the distribution of income assume that an organization exists which allocates rewards in accordance with their productivity. Thus this problem of metering is usually assumed away in economics. In fact this is a big problem because if the economic organization meters well productivity is increased, whereas if it meters badly productivity is reduced. The problem is implicit in the discussion of Chapter 5, but it is of sufficient importance to warrant brief discussion here.

Economics has implicitly recognized that problems of team production exist in firms. In particular it recognizes that individuals might shirk, but it does not specifically handle the problem of monitoring performance which somehow got tacked on to the theory. In principle there was no reason why the neoclassical theory of the firm should not include monitoring and supervision as one of the inputs. It was also well within the scope of the neoclassical theory to show that, in the presence of policing, monitoring, or metering costs, each individual might be induced to take leisure "excessive" (i.e., nonpecuniary reward)[7]. Because taking it easy will have a smaller effect on his realized rate of substitution between output and leisure than on the true rate of substitution. Similarly, the marginal rules for optimal quantity of a policing input would be the same as for any other input[8].

In short, Alchian and Demsetz's analysis by developing the notion of team production is an extension and clarification of earlier work in economics, including that of Coase. Thus according to them the firm emerges because of the fact that extra output is provided by team production, and that, however, success depends on being able to "manage" the team so that metering problems and the attendant shirking are overcome. The firm in economics is seen as being able to solve these problems because its entrepreneur is able to estimate marginal productivities of inputs, and able to organize and direct them so as to obtain the benefits of team production. Thus, like Coase, Alchian and Demsetz provide a *raison d'être* for the firm. In particular Alchian and Demsetz are able to provide two necessary conditions for the emergence of the firm:

1.   The fact that productivity can be increased by team production – a technique for which it is costly directly to measure the marginal outputs of the cooperating inputs.

2.   It is economical to estimate marginal productivity by observing or specifying input behaviour.

The contributions of Coase, and Alchian and Demsetz are important in providing a basis for examination of all kinds of firms, whether hypothetical or real. For example, it should be noted that any of the real firms mentioned earlier face these kinds of problems. They have to decide how big their operation should be, which means that they have to decide when to use the market or do it themselves. They constantly face problems of metering and organization, and so on.

The above analyses of the firm while arising out of neoclassical economics and using the neoclassical notion of the "margin" are related to actual firms. They are also related to hypothetical firms, in that they regard the firm as a device in the price mechanism which is exactly how it is regarded in neoclassical economic theory. The firm in neoclassical economics is a primitive device for turning inputs into outputs. It does this either by its own internal operations or by a combination of its own internal operations and the use of the price mechanism. In contrast to the Coase/Alchian/Demsetz firm, however, the theoretical firm of neoclassical economics does not have to correspond to any actual firm. This point is made forcibly by Machlup (1967, p. 9), in his presidential address to the American Economic Association, with reference to what he calls "misplaced concreteness". "To confuse the firm as a theoretical construct with the firm as an empirical concept, that is, to confuse a heuristic fiction with a real organization is to commit the 'fallacy of misplaced concreteness'. This fallacy consists in using theoretical symbols as though they had direct observable, concrete meaning."

At the risk of labouring the point it is perhaps worth noting a few of the methodological issues involved, as described by Nagel (1963). Theoretical symbols, or "theoretical terms" as Nagel calls them, are not observable. By definition, they correspond to nothing actual. In the case of perfect competition, the word "firm" is used in the sense of a theoretical term, just as in later chapters of this book theoretical terms like "perfectly divisible commodity" will be employed.

While such issues of methodology are under examination it might also be worthwhile pointing out the nature of the abstractions employed in the theory set out in this book. Assumptions will be made that are unrealistic because they are incomplete descriptions of an object: as in physical science where chemists, when describing the reactions between substances indicate only the general or repeatable characteristics of the substances concerned, e.g., the weight of a specimen. Similarly, the assumption that firms maximize profits is arguably unrealistic in this sense, because it abstracts the common and crucial elements from the mass of things surrounding "real" firms and permits valid predictions on the basis of these common and crucial elements alone.

Thus in answer to the question which prompted this section — "What is the difference between the theory of the firm and real world firms?" — it can be argued that, on the one hand, there is the case of the purely theoretical construct with no correspondence to actual firms and, on the other hand, there is the theorizing by Coase and others which relates to actual firms. This has important implications for what follows and for the approach taken here. Depending on the problem involved, the firm in economic theory may be regarded in a number of ways. Although this book is called *Theory of the Firm*, it will be apparent that it is concerned with the discussion of several *theories* of the firm. In so far as there is a unity amongst the theories discussed, and to the extent that this unity is developed in the text, there is a justification for striving for the unity implied by the title *Theory of the Firm*.

1.2 The implications of the theory of the firm for firms and public policy

Section 1.1 has been concerned primarily with positive analysis of the firm which includes the prediction of prices, firm, and industry behaviour. As such it might be relevant to firms in attempting to throw light on the environment in which they operate, e.g., whether it is competitive, or what will be the effects of a unilateral price increase by one firm. It will also be of interest to government in that government may wish to predict the effects on prices of say increased taxes on profits, or a law regarding minimum wages. Additionally, government, and to a lesser extent firms, will be concerned with the normative implications of the theory of the firm.

The traditional normative role of the theory of the firm is due to Adam Smith with his notion of firms striving for their own ends (maximum profits) yet, through the invisible hand of competition, producing a state of affairs which maximize benefits to society. This theorem about decentralized competitive systems is very important in that it shows the design of a system which achieves one definition of social optimality[9].

From this famous example the importance of the theory of the firm in normative analysis can be seen. It is clear that Adam Smith noted how and when the behaviour of the firm resulted in an efficient allocation of resources. This problem, in its simplest and most famous form, is still the major problem of the firm in normative analysis. Government still has to deal with this problem. Welfare economics has developed considerably since the time of Adam Smith. For simplicity, one view is adopted here, namely that the government knows what objectives it wishes to achieve, and can make all the value assumptions regarding income distribution, etc. Thus at the limit, the government specifies an objective function for the economy, the *social welfare function*. It then needs to know when the behaviour of the firm will result in an efficient allocation of resources as defined by the social welfare function.

In complex mixed economies these become difficult questions to answer, especially when the range of firms, and other productive agents — e.g., nationalized industries, and non-profit institutions like hospitals and government agencies — is so great. Thus the study of firms and the development of theories is relevant in this normative context. Examples of the kinds of government policy where firms are involved and the role of theories of the firm in this context are given in Chapter 7. Also noted in Chapter 7 is the tendency of government to involve itself with more areas of economic activity. For example the government's preoccupation with growth of the whole economy makes study of the growth of the firm important in this context.

The tendency for firms to develop and to increase their power and influence also creates problems of government control. In growing large firms create ways of controlling their environment, e.g., by political means, by advertising, by innovation, and by mergers. To some extent, the theory, like government policy, is lagging behind events. Developments in firms' activities to control their environment are placing great strains on both government's ability and that of economists to state with much precision how the behaviour of firms will affect optimal resource allocation. Areas, such as those mentioned above, are, to a considerable extent, speculative. They are still to be absorbed within the body of the theory of the firm. Thus, despite considerable developments in these areas, many of which are empirical, e.g., in advertising and in innovation, very little discussion of these topics will be presented in this book which attempts a more basic approach[10].

Clearly government, firms, and industry are likely to have an interest in the theory of the firm for various reasons including those given in this section. In addition, others will be interested and potentially might gain from a study of the theory of the firm. These include management scientists, engineers, accountants, and lawyers who might gain from the broad strategic and tactical overall view of the firm which the theory of the firm can provide. This would enable them to place their own activities in the context of the role of the firm.

1.3   Plan of the book

The theory of the firm in economics has been the subject of much controversy over the years. It might therefore prove useful as an introduction to what follows to outline very briefly some of the major features of this controversy.

It is quite easy to overemphasize the controversy and forget the substantial measure of agreement. For example, Nordquist (1965, p. 33) seems to be overemphasizing the controversy when he says, "Like an ill-fated ship, the theory of the firm came under fire almost immediately after being launched and subsequently became the subject of one round of criticism after another, virtually without rest." However, this book, like most textbooks, will concentrate upon what seems to be agreed upon and such constructive developments as are in process.

Until the 1920s the neoclassical theory of the firm, with its emphasis on perfect competition, reigned supreme. The firm, like the consumer, was regarded as one of a large number of producers, who individually, because of insignificant size, could not affect market price. True some important dissenting voices had been raised, especially the elegant mathematical exposition of a non-competitive market of Cournot (1938), but the impact had been slight. Progress had been made on the nature of production and the determinants of supply by Marshall (1920). However, his approach, while allowing for the existence of increasing returns, paradoxically insisted upon the widespread application of perfect competition. The dilemma had to be faced — Sraffa (1926) and the subsequent controversy bringing it out quite clearly — that there was an inconsistency between the notion of perfect competition and increasing returns. This paved the way for considerations of market morphologies that allowed the supremacy of perfect competition to be relegated to that of an extreme case. Considera-tion of cases at the other extreme, namely monopoly, became very important and oligopoly theory had got off the ground almost 100 years after it had been conceived by Cournot. With the increased significance of the individual firm in the market which is implied by oligopolistic and monopolistic market situations, the attention was now directed at the firm rather than the industry. This led to questioning of the profit maximiza-tion assumption. As the firm in monopoly would usually make above normal profits more or less automatically, what was the incentive for him to maximize profits? Hicks (1935, p. 8) was one of the first to make this point. "It seems not at all likely that people in monopolistic positions will very often be people with sharply subjective costs; if this is so, they are likely to exploit their advantage much more by not bothering to get very near the position of maximum profit, than by straining themselves to get very close to it. The best of all monopoly profits is a quiet life." Much of the work that followed Hicks was of this kind of questioning variety which, with the possible exception of Scitovsky (1943), posed questions rather than supplied answers in the form of advances in the theory of the firm. This is not to imply that significant questions were not asked. As early as 1941 Tintner started to raise questions about the effects of un-certainty on the profit maximization assumption. Questions came from empirical as well as theoretical studies. For example, Berle and Means

(1932) raised questions about the effect of ownership and control on the incentive to maximize profits by large companies. Meanwhile Hall and Hitch (1939), in a study of UK companies' pricing policies, came across the "full cost" pricing principle, which was apparently entirely different from the marginalist approach of the firm in neoclassical economics. This erupted into the "marginalist controversy" after the Second World War, where a group of economists, especially Machlup (1946) defended, with great vigour the attacks on the theory of the firm implied by the full-cost approach. This controversy was long and remained at the centre of the stage until interest in the theory of the firm was aroused by the advances of Baumol, Cyert and March, Marris, and Williamson in the 1960s. It was only then that feasible theoretical alternatives to the neoclassical firm started to appear which answered, at least partially, some of the questions posed by the earlier critics.

This book will not aim to cover all the ground described above. Its aim will be to set out the neoclassical theory of the firm to provide a benchmark against which to measure alternative theories. It will not therefore engage in long commentaries on the various controversies described above. It will not avoid controversy entirely in that it will attempt to state some of the problems of alternative theories and the scope for future developments in the theory of the firm.

Many of the advances that have been achieved in the theory of the firm have, like recent advances in other branches of economics, been due to the use of powerful mathematical techniques. Additionally, the theory of the firm has been influenced by developments in behavioural science and management science which have led economists to return to serious examination of the internal operation and efficiency of firms. These kinds of influences are at work in the mathematical programming developments discussed in Chapter 3 and the discussion of the "new" theories of the firm in Chapter 5.

Chapters 2, 3, and 4 examine the neoclassical theory of the firm and market structure and the programming approach to the firm. Chapter 2 examines the technology and costs side of the firm and, for the most part, assumes that the firm has to accept price as given and adjusts its output accordingly. The analysis is essentially neoclassical, assuming that the firm aims at maximizing profits. Chapter 3 also assumes that firms maximize profits and compares the neoclassical approach of Chapter 2 with the programming analysis of the firm. Chapter 4 is concerned with market structures and the role of (principally neoclassical) economic theory in the analysis and prediction of market behaviour.

Chapter 5 critically examines the profit maximization assumption in the light of some recent developments in the theory of the firm. For lack of a better term these are called "new" theories of the firm or "alternative" theories of the firm. The influence of behavioural science and management science in these marginal theories is very important and will become apparent in the course of the chapter. A comparison between these theories and the neoclassical profit maximizing theory is made.

Chapter 6 is concerned with more developments and influences on the theory of the firm which unlike the "new" theories in Chapter 5, are not easily categorized under the heading of motivation. Considerations of general equilibrium, uncertainty, and growth of the firm are discussed. Considerations of uncertainty and dynamic analysis in the theory of the firm have important implications for that theory. Some of these are discussed.

Finally Chapter 7, by way of summary and conclusion, attempts to show the importance of the theory of the firm in positive and normative economics. In examining in some detail the implications for public policy of the theory of the firm this chapter unashamedly reflects the author's own personal views on the subject.

Notes

1.   The approach of searching for "generality" of this kind is not adopted here. Thus the present book is in contrast to that of Hicks (1946) who says of his own volume,

This is a work on theoretical economics, considered as the logical analysis of an economic system of private enterprise, without any inclusion of reference to institutional controls. For I consider the pure logical analysis of capitalism to be a task in itself, while the survey of economic institutions is best carried on by the methods such as those of the economic historian.

2.   Coase's paper and the paper by Alchian and Demsetz are important in that they concern themselves with internal resource allocation by firms. Leibenstein (1966) is another economist who has been concerned with the efficiency with which firms allocate resources within themselves. He coins the phrase X-efficiency for this kind of internal efficiency within firms. Usually, economists implicitly assume that the firm is X-efficient, and are only concerned with the familiar concept of allocative efficiency, which is concerned with how the price mechanism allocates resources. (This subject

will come up again in the course of the book, for example, in some detail in Chapters 5 and 7.)

3.   See Coase (1952, p. 333). One of the interesting developments in real firms is the use of management science. Paradoxically the effect of this is for to encourage the use in some large firms of systems of allocation which stimulate market processes. For example, a firm might give its managers "shadow" prices of certain resources. The managers then work to maximize profits on the basis of these. It is of course an open question whether such internal markets within firms operate as efficiently as markets outside the firm would do.

4.   The contract of employment is not entirely specified. Obviously, the powers of the employer are limited and the duties of the employee are not completely specified. This is the principal difference between employment and slavery.

5.   Later discussion of advances in the theory of the firm (see pp. 109–11) examines the control loss phenomenon. Coase's explanations should be compared with those of Williamson (1970) who shows how firms have tended to change their organizational form in response to problems of control loss.

6.   This part at first glance may appear trite. However, something close to sabotage may occur in less severe forms where one group of workers feels that it is not being rewarded according to its productivity. This may result in its undertaking, say, a highly damaging strike.

7.   This is because taking it easy will have a smaller effect on the individual's realized rate of substitution between output and leisure than on the true rate of substitution (for the firm).

8.   Sometimes almost nothing is devoted to policing as, to cite the example given by Alchian and Demsetz (1972, pp. 780–1), in a university. However, the extra costs of identifying each individual's abuse of the system are greater than the savings from reducing faculty "turpitudinal peccadiloes". Because of this "amenity-seizing", money wages tend to be reduced. It does not follow, however, that the combination of money wage and ease of work is the optimal one. As trade is not possible it seems most likely that some other combinations would prove to be optimal. Thus if a costless method of policing could be derived individuals could then be given the opportunity perhaps to trade amenities for income.

9.   This is, of course, a now famous property of perfect competition. It must, therefore, always play a unique role in the theory of welfare economics. For a discussion see Mishan (1960) and Graaf (1957) for just two of many analyses of this subject.

10.   For examples of empirical work in advertising see Cowling (1972).

2

Production, cost and equilibrium: neoclassical theory of the firm

In neoclassical theory the firm is seen as a theoretical construct, not corresponding to any actual firm, and is seen as a primitive device for transforming inputs into output. The firm is under the control of the entrepreneur, who, subject to various technical rules specified in his production function, combines inputs to produce output so that the excess of revenue over cost is maximized. This is the so-called profit maximization assumption which plays such an important part in the theory of the firm. Another aspect of neoclassical economics, which is worth noting, is the nature of the analytical methods employed by neoclassical theory. It employs almost exclusively classical calculus. It assumes continuous functions where second derivatives exist. This implies the use of certain theoretical terms like "perfectly divisible commodity" and "perfectly divisible input"[1].

The fundamental motivation then of the entrepreneur in neoclassical economics is to extract maximum profit from his activities of purchasing inputs, and combining them to produce output. The problems involved are broken down into their component parts in the sections which follow. Section 2.1 examines the nature of the production function with consideration given to homogeneous production functions. Section 2.2 shows how the optimal combination of inputs is determined from the production function. Section 2.3 shows how cost functions are derived from production functions. Section 2.4 introduces revenue considerations and shows how equilibrium of the firm is achieved. Section 2.5 discusses extensions of the model to include multiproduct firms and joint product firms. Finally, section 2.6 examines the comparative statics of the firm.

2.1 The production function
The production function is an engineering or technological relationship

between quantity of output and quantity of inputs. As will be noted in Chapter 3, it assumes away the often complex problem of determining the maximum output from given quantities of input. Perhaps the most common elementary type of a production function is the type which relates two variable inputs X_1 and X_2 and a single output (Q). In this case the production function states the relationship with technology unchanging between quantity of output (q) and quantities X_1 and X_2 of the variable inputs.

$$q = f(x_1, x_2) \qquad\qquad [2.1]$$

An example of a production function like [2.1] is given in Fig. 2.1. As this production function (with two variable inputs) is represented by a

Fig. 2.1

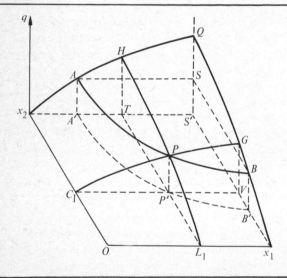

three-dimensional diagram it is called a *production surface*. Any point on the surface represents output. If a perpendicular is dropped the quantities of inputs required to produce this output can be determined. For example, if a perpendicular is dropped from P to P' the quantities of x_1 and x_2 can be read off as $OC_1 (= L_1 P')$ and $OL_1 (= C_1 P')$.

Another way of looking at a production surface is to assume that x_2 is held constant at C_1. By starting at C_1 and tracing the quantity of output at this level of C_1 it is possible to derive the curve $C_1 PG$ which gives the output, with x_2 held constant at C_1, that arises as a result of using in-

Fig. 2.2

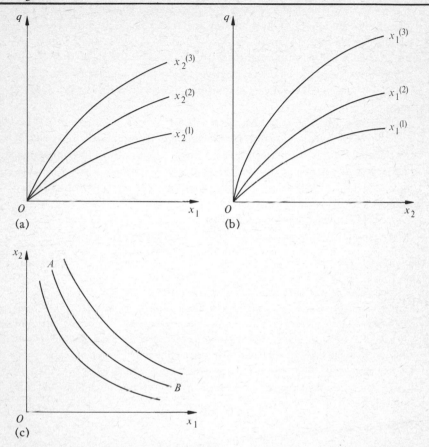

(a)

(b)

(c)

creating amounts of x_1. An analogous curve for x_2 held constant at L_1 is shown by L_1PH. Curves like these are called total product curves or productivity curves and are given by

$$q = f(x_1, x_2^o) \qquad [2.2a]$$

where $x_2^o = OC_1$ in this case, but more generally any fixed value of x_2 and

$$q = f(x_1^o, x_2) \qquad [2.2b]$$

For any fixed value x_1^o of X_1, productivity curves are often drawn in two-dimensional space. A family of such curves is shown in Figs. 2.2a and 2.2b. Figure 2.2a relates changes in total product (Q) to X_1 with X_2 held constant. In Fig. 2.2a curve $Ox_2^{(2)}$ — with $x_2^{(2)}$ of X_2 — is exactly analogous to C_1PG with OC_1 of capital of Fig. 2.1. Curve $x_2^{(1)}$ corresponds to $x_2^{(1)}$ of X_2 which is less than $x_2^{(2)}$ and which would correspond to a lower cross-section of the production surface in Fig. 2.1. Similarly $x_2^{(3)}$, which corresponds to more of X_1, offers a higher total product. In Fig. 2.2b, a corresponding argument applies to X_2 with X_1 held constant. Notice how the slope of the productivity curve becomes flatter as more of the input is used. This reflects diminishing marginal returns to the variable input.

Isoquants (see Fig. 2.2c) are also derived from a production surface. Point P on the production surface corresponds to the output level PP'. If this output level is maintained around the production surface and perpendiculars of equal height dropped an isoquant $A'P'B'$ is traced out on the input (X_1, X_2) plane. This is illustrated in Fig. 2.2c along with three more isoquants which form an isoquant map.

An isoquant map can be derived from [2.1] by taking a given level of output and treating it as a parameter q^o.

$$q^o = f(x_1, x_2) \tag{2.3}$$

Shape of the production surface (Function)
Production functions are usually assumed to have convex (to the origin) isoquants. Thus production functions themselves will normally, but not necessarily, be concave (or strictly concave)[2]. Notice that, in the case of the neoclassical theory, concavity (or strict concavity) is not necessary. All that is assumed is that the production surface is concave over a range, in which case the following second order conditions hold for the two variable input case:

$$f_{11} \leqslant 0 \quad f_{22} \leqslant 0$$

$$\begin{vmatrix} f_{11} & f_{12} \\ f_{21} & f_{22} \end{vmatrix} \geqslant 0$$

Input substitution
From the isoquant map it is possible to examine the way one input can be substituted for another. Using a particular isoquant the rate at which one input must be substituted for another to maintain output can be derived. The negative of the slope of the isoquant gives the number of units of x_2 that must be substituted per unit of x_{11} in order to hold output constant. This is called the marginal rate of technical substitution − MRTS.

MRTS can be derived from the production function [2.1] by taking the total differential

$$dq = f_1 \, dx_1 + f_2 \, dx_2 \tag{2.4}$$

and equating it to zero (because output is unchanged along any isoquant making $dq = 0$) to give

$$-\frac{dx_2}{dx_1} = \frac{f_1}{f_2} = \text{MRTS} \qquad [2.5]$$

where

$$f_1 = \frac{\partial q}{\partial x_1} \quad \text{and} \quad f_2 = \frac{\partial q}{\partial x_2}$$

f_1 and f_2 are marginal products of X_1 and X_2 respectively since they represent changes in output arising from additional applications of inputs X_1 and X_2. Thus MRTS is seen to be equal to the ratio of the two marginal products.

Elasticity of substitution
The rate at which substitution takes place is called the *elasticity of substitution* and is given by σ. It is defined as a measure of the relative responsiveness of the input ratio to given proportional changes in MRTS or

$$\sigma = \Delta\left(\frac{x_2}{x_1}\right) \div \frac{\Delta\text{MRTS}}{\text{MRTS}} \Bigg/ \left(\frac{x_2}{x_1}\right)$$

$$= \frac{d(x_2/x_1)}{d(f_1/f_2)} \cdot \frac{f_1/f_2}{x_2/x_1} \qquad [2.6]$$

Short run and long run
The analysis has so far assumed that it is possible to vary the quantity of inputs, x_1 and x_2, at will. Implicit in this approach has been the assumption that another input whose quantity could not be changed *in the short run* was used with X_1 and X_2. The short run is defined as that period when one or more inputs are fixed. The long run is defined as that period when all inputs are variable. The production functions described above describe the production possibilities of the firm in the short run. If the amount of the fixed input is changed the form of the production function is changed.

Examples of production functions
Two famous examples of production functions are the Cobb–Douglas production function and the constant elasticity of substitution (CES) function.

The Cobb—Douglas function is given by

$$q = Ax_1^{\alpha} x_2^{1-\alpha} \qquad [2.7]$$

where $\quad 0 < \alpha < 1$

It is homogeneous in degree one (linear homogeneous), and implies constant returns to scale: if all inputs are expanded in the same proportion, output is expanded in that proportion. If both x_1 and x_2 are increased by λ then output is increased by λ. This is shown below.

$$\begin{aligned} f(\lambda x_1, \lambda x_2) &= A\lambda^{\alpha} x_1^{\alpha} \lambda^{1-\alpha} x_2^{1-\alpha} \\ &= (\lambda^{\alpha+1-\alpha}) A x_1^{\alpha} x_2^{1-\alpha} \\ &= \lambda A x_1^{\alpha} x_2^{1-\alpha} \\ &= \lambda f(x_1, x_2) \\ &= \lambda q \qquad [2.8] \end{aligned}$$

Other important features of the Cobb—Douglas function are that the marginal products of both inputs are homogeneous in degree zero, and that the marginal product of each input declines as that input only is increased.

The Cobb—Douglas function is a special type of CES function with elasticity of substitution equal to one. The general CES function is homogeneous and has constant elasticity of substitution,

$$q = A[\alpha x_1^{-\rho} + (1 - \alpha)x_2^{-\rho}]^{-h/\rho} \qquad [2.9]$$

where h is the degree of homogeneity. The elasticity of substitution is

$$\sigma = \frac{1}{1 + \rho} \qquad [2.10]$$

This can be illustrated for the original CES function as developed by Arrow, Chenery, Minhas, and Solow (1961) which is homogeneous in degree one, viz. $h = 1$. From marginal products[3] of

$$f_1 = \frac{\partial q}{\partial x_1} = \frac{\alpha}{A^{\rho}} \left(\frac{q}{x_1}\right)^{\rho+1} \qquad f_2 = \frac{\partial q}{\partial x_2} = \frac{1 - \alpha}{A^{\rho}} \left(\frac{q}{x_2}\right)^{\rho+1}$$

$$\frac{f_1}{f_2} = \frac{\alpha}{1 - \alpha} \left(\frac{x_2}{x_1}\right)^{\rho+1} \qquad [2.11]$$

$$\frac{\dfrac{f_1}{f_2}}{\dfrac{x_2}{x_1}} = \frac{\dfrac{\alpha}{1 - \alpha} \left(\dfrac{x_2}{x_1}\right)^{\rho+1}}{\dfrac{x_2}{x_1}} = \frac{\alpha}{1 - \alpha} \left(\frac{x_2}{x_1}\right)^{\rho} \qquad [2.12]$$

differentiating [2.11] with respect of $\dfrac{x_2}{x_1}$ yields

$$\frac{d\left(\dfrac{f_1}{f_2}\right)}{d\left(\dfrac{x_2}{x_1}\right)} = (\rho + 1)\,\frac{\alpha}{1 - \alpha}\left(\frac{x_2}{x_1}\right)^{\rho} \qquad\qquad [2.13]$$

Substituting [2.12] and [2.13] into [2.6] yields

$$\sigma = \frac{\dfrac{f_1}{f_2}}{\dfrac{x_2}{x_1}}\,\frac{d\left(\dfrac{x_2}{x_1}\right)}{d\left(\dfrac{f_1}{f_2}\right)} = \frac{1}{\rho + 1}$$

It should be noted that $\rho \geqslant -1$.

2.2 Optimizing behaviour

The technical relationship as described by the production function does not tell the firm what combination of resources it should employ to achieve a given level of output. It merely shows the infinity of combinations of inputs which will produce a given output. However, when input prices are known these can be used along with the production function to arrive at the optimal input combination for a given output.

Minimizing cost for a given output
Suppose the firm faces input prices of r_1 and r_2 and that these are constant irrespective of the amount it buys of these inputs. The firm may either minimize the cost of producing a given output or maximize the output for a given cost. The former is shown below. The latter is shown in note 5.

In the two-input case cost may be represented by a straight line. As x_1 and x_2 can be purchased for r_1 and r_2 per unit it follows that total cost of purchasing any amount of x_1 and x_2 is given by a straight line.

$$C = r_1 x_1 + r_2 x_2 \ldots \qquad\qquad [2.14]$$

Isocost lines can be derived from [2.14] by treating C as a parameter C^o. A set of isocost lines is drawn in Fig. 2.3 together with a given output q^o. Costs of producing this output are clearly minimized at B on isocost line $C^{(2)}$ which is the lowest line touching q^o. At B it is noted that the slope of isoquant q is equal to the slope of the isocost line. Thus it is clear from the

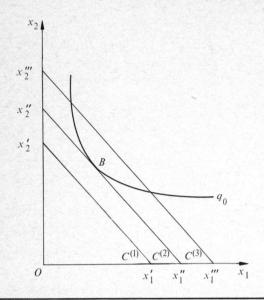

previous definition [2.5] that, at B, the negative of the slope of the isocost line is equal to the MRTS. From this it can be noted that MRTS is equal to the ratio of the factor prices viz:

$$\text{MRTS} = -\frac{dx_2}{dx_1} = \frac{f_1}{f_2} = \frac{r_1}{r_2} \cdot \cdot \cdot \cdot \quad\quad [2.15]$$

Solving [2.14] for x_2 yields

$$x_2 = \frac{C}{r_2} - \frac{r_1}{r_2} x_1$$

which has a slope of $-\dfrac{r_1}{r_2}$.

Thus expression [2.15] immediately follows from this[4].

The result may be obtained directly by simply minimizing the cost function $C = r_1 x_1 + r_2 x_2$ subject to the constraint that output is fixed at q^o or $q^o = f(x_1, x_2)$ where $f(x_1, x_2)$ is the production function. Setting up a Lagrangian

$$L = r_1 x_1 + r_2 x_2 + \mu[q^o - f(x_1, x_2)]$$

and setting partial derivatives with respect to x_1, x_2 and equal to zero yields:

$$\frac{\partial L}{\partial x_1} = r_1 - \mu f_1 = 0 \tag{2.16}$$

$$\frac{\partial L}{\partial x_2} = r_2 - \mu f_2 = 0 \tag{2.17}$$

$$\frac{\partial L}{\partial \mu} = q^0 - f(x_1, x_2) = 0 \tag{2.18}$$

Moving the price terms to the right and dividing [2.16] by [2.17] yields

$$\frac{f_1}{f_2} = \frac{r_1}{r_2} = \text{MRTS} \ldots \tag{2.19}[5]$$

The meaning of the Lagrange multiplier, μ, is interesting since it represents the change in total cost which results from a change in output, i.e., $\frac{dC}{dq}$ which is defined as marginal cost in section 2.3.

If C is treated as a variable for the moment it follows from [2.14] that

$$dC = r_1 \, dx_1 + r_2 \, dx_2 \tag{2.20}$$

if, from [2.16] and [2.17] $r_1 = \mu f_1$ and $r_2 = \mu f_2$ are substituted into [2.20] it follows that

$$dC = \mu f_1 \, dx_1 + \mu f_2 \, dx_2$$
$$= \mu(f_1 \, dx_1 + f_2 \, dx_2) \tag{2.21}$$

If [2.21] is divided by [2.4], the differential of the production function

$$\frac{dC}{dq} = \frac{\mu(f_1 \, dx_1 + f_2 \, dx_2)}{(f_1 \, dx_1 + f_2 \, dx_2)} = \mu \tag{2.22}$$

which is marginal cost.

Expansion path
Suppose that the locus of points of tangency like B in Fig. 2.3 are drawn in Fig. 2.4 as $OABC$, this represents the input combinations which a firm would choose to correspond to outputs given by, e.g., q^0, q^1, q^2.

The expansion path is given by an implicit function $g(x_1, x_2) = 0$ for which the conditions [2.19] are fulfilled. (Exercise 1 requires that the expansion path for a Cobb—Douglas and a CES function be derived.)

Fig. 2.4

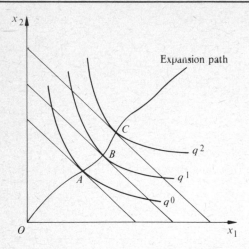

Expansion paths will obviously start at the origin and can be any shape. With a homogeneous production function they are linear. However, a linear expansion path does not necessarily imply a homogeneous production function. Take the case of a production function given by $q = Ax_1^4 x_2^4 - Bx_1^5 x_2^5$.

In line with Fig. 2.4 the ratio of the marginal products is formed (MRTS)

$$\frac{f_1}{f_2} = \frac{4Ax_1^3 x_2^4 - 5Bx_1^4 x_2^5}{4Ax_1^4 x_2^3 - 5Bx_1^5 x_2^4} = \frac{x_2(4Ax_1^3 x_2^3 - 5Bx_1^4 x_2^4)}{x_1(4Ax_1^3 x_2^3 - 5Bx_1^4 x_2^4)} = \frac{x_2}{x_1}$$

This is then equal to the ratio of the input prices (isocostline)

$$\frac{x_2}{x_1} = \frac{r_1}{r_2}$$

which rearranged in the form of an implicit function yields the linear expansion path

$$r_2 x_2 - r_1 x_1 = 0.$$

2.3 Cost functions

From the information provided by points of tangency with isocost curves and isoquants it is possible to construct a total-cost function which relates total cost to the level of output. As implied in section 2.2, how output was produced depended on whether the firm was in a long-run or a short-run situation. Similarly, short-run and long-run costs may differ. Initially short-run costs will be examined. Long-run costs will then be examined. It should be clear that long-run costs obviously include short-run costs, in the sense that every long-run position has a short-run position corresponding to it.

Opportunity cost

Previously, the term cost has only been implicit in the analysis in that the input prices r_1 and r_2 were assumed to constitute costs in relation to the isocost line. Nothing was said about *opportunity cost*, which is the usual term used by economists to denote costs. The opportunity cost of producing a unit of commodity Z is the amount of commodity Y that must be sacrificed in order to produce Z rather than Y. Input prices r_1 and r_2 were assumed to reflect opportunity costs in that they represented what the firm had to pay for X_1 and X_2 in order to acquire them. The notion of opportunity cost presents few difficulties if it entails simply outlays like r_1 and r_2 above. However, opportunity cost needs to take into account not just outlays or the explicit costs when the firm purchases resources. It also has to take into account implicit costs which would include, for example, the alternative interest the firm could earn on capital invested in the firm and alternative income which the entrepreneur could earn for his time and labour in the firm. Pure economic profit, henceforth referred to simply as profit, would therefore be any excess of total receipts over the sum of all explicit and implicit costs.

Short run costs

As mentioned in section 2.1 the short run is that period of time in which the quantities of certain inputs cannot be varied at all. Thus, regardless of the level of output, these inputs cannot be changed. Corresponding to these fixed inputs are costs that do not vary as output is varied in the short run. These costs are called fixed costs and are the sum of explicit fixed costs and implicit costs. However, as noted above in section 2.2, in the two variable input case the two inputs x_1 and x_2 can be varied. The variable costs are simply $r_1 x_1 + r_2 x_2$ which are dependent only on the amounts of x_1 and x_2 used. Total cost would then be variable cost + fixed cost, K or

$$C = K + r_1 x_1 + r_2 x_2 \qquad [2.23]$$

From the study of the production function in section 2.2 it is clear that only points on the expansion path are considered by the firm since all other points at the same level of expenditure correspond to less output for the same cost. It is thus possible to derive the total-cost function, which is simply total cost as a function of output.

At each level of expenditure there is a maximum output (the point of tangency with the opportunity line, the point on the expansion path). This level of output, using the isoquant, can be related to the cost (from the opportunity line) plus fixed costs to give the function total-cost (TC) which simply relates cost to output. TC is derived therefore by taking [2.23], the production function, and the expansion path. This system of three equations in four variables is reduced to a single equation in which cost is stated as an explicit function of output and the cost of the fixed input[6].

$$TC = \Psi(q) + K \qquad\qquad [2.24]$$

At the risk of labouring the point, every cost-output combination in [2.24] can be obtained in four steps:

1. Select a point on the expansion path.

2. Substitute the input levels corresponding to this point into the production function to yield the output.

3. Multiply the levels of each input (x_1, x_2) by the input prices r_1 and r_2 to give the total variable cost of this output level.

4. Add the fixed cost (K).

A number of other types of cost are derived from TC. These are *average* cost and marginal cost. Average cost (AC) is simply TC divided by output (q), i.e.,

$$AC = \frac{TC}{q} = \frac{\Psi(q) + K}{q}$$

$$= \frac{\Psi(q)}{q} + \frac{K}{q} \qquad\qquad [2.25]$$

The first of these expressions $\dfrac{\Psi(q)}{q}$ = AVC = average variable cost.

The second of these expressions $\dfrac{K}{q}$ = AFC = average fixed cost.

Marginal cost is the addition to total cost attributable to producing one unit of output, or

$$TC_n - TC_{n-1} = MC = \text{marginal cost} \qquad\qquad [2.26]$$

Where TC_n = total cost of producing n units.

In view of the fact that the neoclassical analysis uses continuous functions and therefore perfectly divisible units it follows that MC can be regarded as the rate of change of total cost or[7]

$$MC = \frac{dTC}{dq} = \Psi'(q) \qquad [2.27]$$

Geometrically TC is given in Fig. 2.5. In addition, TVC (total variable cost or $\Psi(q)$) and TFC (total fixed cost or K) are shown. Obvious TC and TVC are parallel as the distance K separates them.

Fig. 2.5

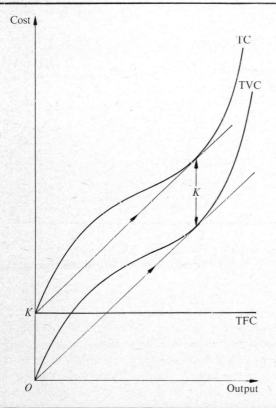

AC, MC, AFC and AVC are drawn in Fig. 2.6. Except for AFC which is a rectangular hyperbola they are drawn in the familiar U-shape to reflect the neoclassical views on costs and the production functions described above. Thus marginal costs decrease, reach a minimum, and then increase[8].

Fig. 2.6

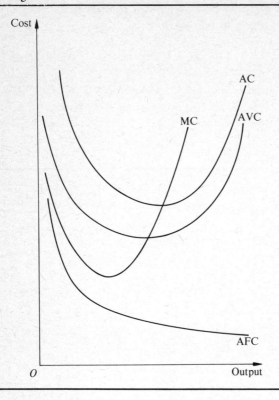

Just above its own minimum point in Fig. 2.5 MC cuts AVC at its minimum point; at a slightly larger output it cuts AC also at its minimum[9].

Long-run costs

As mentioned above, the long run is that period of time of such length that the quantities of all inputs may be varied. The long run is essentially a planning horizon. All production takes place in the short run. "Long run" refers to the fact that firms can plan ahead and choose which "short run" situation they will operate in the future. Thus a *long run* situation is one where the firm can choose from among all short run situations. Before an investment is made — in the case above before K units have been invested in the fixed factor — the firm is in a long run situation. It can choose to invest any amount in the fixed factor. However, in the situation described above this decision had been made. The amount of the fixed factor had been determined at K in the case discussed above and the firm has to operate within this. It might be most helpful therefore to think of a firm *planning* in the long run and operating in the short run. (An example of this point is given at the end of this chapter to indicate possible application of this analysis to electricity supply.)

Short run and long run cost curves
The above points regarding long run and short run cost might become clearer by means of an example. It is assumed in Fig. 2.7 that the firm has the choice of three amounts, K_1, K_2, and K_3 of the fixed factor (where $K_1 < K_2 < K_3$). If it chooses K_1 it gets onto short run average cost SAC_1; if it chooses K_2 it gets into SAC_2 (and K_3 onto SAC_3). The dotted part of the SAC curves correspond to situations where a different amount invested in

Fig. 2.7

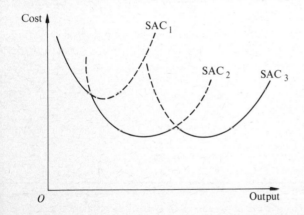

K would result in lower average costs. Thus if the firm in its long run situation is faced with the prospect of investing K_1, K_2, or K_3 its choice depends on what it expects output will be. If it expects output of less than x_1 it will invest K_1. If it expects output of between x_1 and x_2 it will invest K_2 and if it expects output above x_2 it will invest K_3. Once the choice has been made, for example, involving investment of K_2 and output exceeds x_2 the firm can increase output in the short run but only at a cost in excess of what is possible had it made the correct long run decision.

From Fig. 2.7 it is clear that the solid curve is the long run cost curve. If, instead of assuming that only three levels of K could be chosen, it is assumed that K can be continuously varied a continuous "envelope" curve of long-run average cost can be derived. This is done in Fig. 2.8 for an LAC

Fig. 2.8

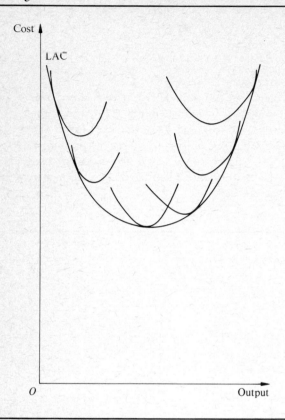

curve and in Fig. 2.9 for a LTC curve. It is clear from both diagrams that the envelope does have the property that it is the minimum cost of any output level. Hence it is sometimes termed optimal scale. These results may be derived more formally by introducing K as a continuous variable in the production function, the cost curve and the expansion path:

$$q = f(x_1, x_2, K)$$
$$C = r_1 x_1 + r_2 x_2 + \Phi(K)$$
$$0 = g(x_1, x_2, K)$$

Thus fixed cost now becomes an increasing function of $K : \Phi'(K) > 0$. If x_1 and x_2 are eliminated the total-cost function as a function of q and K corresponding to [2.24] is derived as

$$TC = \Psi(q, K) + \Phi(K) \tag{2.28}$$

Fig. 2.9

This is not the long-run total-cost curve of a given level of output. In fact the cost function [2.28] corresponds to say cost function $K^{(1)}$ with $K = K^{(1)}$. To derive LTC the envelope needs to be derived from the family of total-cost curves given by [2.28]. This is achieved by writing [2.28] in implicit form and setting its partial derivative with respect to K equal to zero:

$$\text{TC} - \Psi(q, K) - \Phi(K) = G(\text{TC}, q, K) = 0 \qquad [2.29]$$

$$G_K(C, q, K) = 0 \qquad [2.30]$$

and eliminating K from [2.29], [2.30] and solving for TC as a function of q. (The reader is encouraged to solve exercise 9 at the end of this chapter to clarify his understanding of the techniques.)

Long run marginal cost is the derivative with respect to LTC (the envelope in Fig. 2.9). It is obviously itself not an envelope. It is the locus of the points on the short run marginal cost curves (SMC) which correspond to points on the envelope (LAC).

These two methods of deriving LMC (from LTC or LAC) are clearly equivalent since the long-run total-cost curve is tangential to the short-run total-cost curve, thus implying equality of their marginal cost curves. In

Fig. 2.10

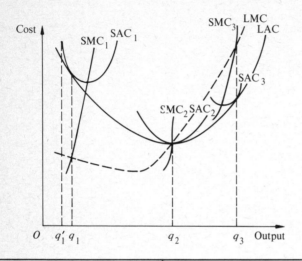

Fig. 2.10 at q_1, LMC = SMC_1 and LAC = SAC_1; and at q_2, LMC = LAC. At outputs less than q_2 (with the U-shaped cost curve) LMC $<$ LAC and at outputs greater than q_2, LMC $>$ LAC. Similarly, for outputs less than optimal scale LMC $>$ SMC. This can be explained by taking some output slightly less than q_1 and noticing what happens if output is expanded to q_1. This implies moving from a point where SAC $>$ LAC to a point where SAC = LAC. Thus the addition to short-run *total*-costs (viz. SMC) must be smaller than the addition to long-run total-costs (viz. LMC). The opposite situation would apply with movements in the opposite direction, i.e., from outputs greater than q_1.

2.4   Revenue and equilibrium

Section 2.3 completes the analysis of production and cost in the neo-classical theory of the firm. However, the neoclassical firm is concerned ultimately not with the solution of problems such as those described above but rather with the maximization of profit. While it is true that the firm must solve all the problems described above if it is to maximize profits, it

must be stressed that the firm cannot maximize profits without simultaneously taking into account cost and revenue. Revenue is what the firm
receives for its output and is here assumed to be a constant price of p per
unit. This corresponds to a perfectly competitive market situation and as
such will be discussed in detail in Chapter 4. At the moment the analysis is
concerned with this elementary case.

The profit (π) function can be formed on the basis of previous
information. It is defined as

$$\pi = pq - C \tag{2.31}$$

which is simply the difference between total revenue and total cost. If the
expressions for $q = f(x_1, x_2)$ and $C = K + r_1x_1 + r_2x_2$ are substituted into
[2.31] the following profit function is derived:

$$\pi = pf(x_1, x_2) - K - r_1x_1 - r_2x_2 \dots \tag{2.32}$$

which, if differentiated, yields

$$\frac{\partial \pi}{\partial x_1} = pf_1 - r_1 = 0$$

$$\frac{\partial \pi}{\partial x_2} = pf_2 - r_2 = 0$$

As f_1 and f_2 are marginal products it follows that the price of each input is
equated to its marginal product multiplied by the price of output (p). The
latter is called value of the marginal product VMP.

Alternatively, and more usually, it is assumed that the problem of
optimal input proportions described in section 2.3 has been solved. The
profit function is then given by

$$\pi = pq - \Psi(q) - K$$

This is differentiated with respect to q and set equal to zero:

$$\frac{\partial \pi}{\partial q} = p - \Psi'(q) = 0$$

or $p = MC$

Thus the firm sets price equal to marginal cost where p is a constant, to
maximize profits. More generally, the rule to maximize profits is stated as:
equate marginal revenue (MR) to marginal cost, where marginal revenue is
the addition to total revenue (TR) from selling one more unit or the
derivative of TR with respect to q, i.e., $\dfrac{dTR}{dq}$. In this case TR $= pq$ and
MR $= p$.

The second-order conditions for maximization of profit require that

$$\frac{d^2 \pi}{dq^2} = -\Psi''(q) < 0$$

which in the case of constant price, p, yields $\dfrac{d^2 C}{dq^2} > 0$.

This is another way of saying that MC is rising at the profit maximizing (or equilibrium) output. This is important, as may be noted in Fig. 2.11, since

Fig. 2.11

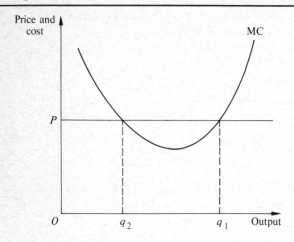

it implies that the marginal cost curve cuts the price line (MR) when marginal cost is rising, that is at q_1. More generally, as can be noted in Fig. 4.10, it can be stated that the marginal cost curve cuts the marginal revenue curve from below. Notice that the second-order conditions make it clear that q_1 is chosen as maximum profit and not q_2 (where first-order conditions are fulfilled) but which actually represents maximum losses.

(The reader is encouraged to check his understanding of this by working example 8 at the end of this chapter.)

2.5   Joint product and multiproduct firms
The production processes discussed above yielded only one output. It is quite possible for a production process to yield more than one output. This is called joint production, and joint production exists when the

production of one commodity entails the production of another commodity, often called a byproduct. Examples of joint production would be wool and mutton, beef and hides, petrol and oil. This should be distinguished from the usual case of the multiproduct firm where a number of products are produced but production of each is independent of the other. The latter is really a generalization of the theory of the firm as so far described: instead of one output and two inputs m outputs and n inputs are discussed.

One input/two outputs joint production
The simplest case of joint production is where a firm uses a single input (X) to produce two outputs (Q_1 and Q_2). There are two cases which can be considered: fixed proportion and variable proportions. The fixed proportions case is simply where a production function always produces a fixed proportion of Q_1 and Q_2. Thus if $q_1/q_2 = 1$, q_1 and q_2 can be treated as a combined commodity with price of $P_c = p_1 + p_2$. Where the firm has to take prices p^1 and p^2 as given, k is then marginal revenue and is simply equated with marginal cost in a manner directly analogous to the case discussed in section 2.4.

The variable proportions case is more complicated. The simplest case of variable proportions is where the firm produces two outputs from a single input, its production function in implicit form being

$$H(q_1, q_2, x) = 0 \qquad [2.33]$$

where q_1, q_2 are quantities of outputs and x is the quantity of the input (X). If [2.33] is solved explicitly for x:

$$x = h(q_1, q_2) \qquad [2.34]$$

The cost of production in terms of X is thus a function of the quantities of outputs q_1 and q_2.

Analogous to the isoquant is the transformation curve which shows the combination of q^1 and q^2 that can be secured by a given amount of X on:

$$x^0 = h(q^1, q^2)$$

In Fig. 2.12 a map of transformation curves is drawn which shows all combinations of outputs q_1 and q_2 that can be produced when x^0, x^1, and x^2 units of input are used. A map of transformation curves is shown with higher curves representing larger amounts of x employed. The slope of the tangent to a point on the transformation curve is the rate at which Q_2 must be sacrificed for Q_1 without varying the input of X. It is called the *marginal rate of transformation* (MRT) and is analogous to the MRS in the way it is derived.

Fig. 2.12

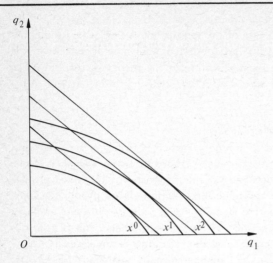

If the total differential of [2.34] is equated to zero (because x^0 = constant):

$$dx = b_1 \, dq_1 + b_2 \, dq_2 = 0 \qquad [2.35]$$

From [2.35] it follows that

$$\text{MRT} = -\frac{dq_2}{dq_1} = \frac{b_1}{b_2} \qquad [2.36]$$

The MRT at a point on the transformation curve equals the ratio of the marginal cost of Q_1 in terms of X to the marginal cost of Q_2 in terms of X at that point. These are shown in Fig. 2.12 corresponding to revenue levels of R^1, R^2, and R^3.

Maximizing revenue subject to a given amount of X

The firm, for a given amount of input X, maximizes revenue. This is analogous to the two input/one output case of minimizing the cost of a given level of output. The firm sells q_1 and q_2 at fixed prices p_1 and p_2 giving revenue (R) of

$$R = p_1 q_1 + p_2 q_2 \qquad [2.37]$$

The linear expression [2.37] will form an *isorevenue line* for each level of R.

Proceeding with the optimization problem involves setting up the Lagrangian:

$$V = p_1 q_1 + p_2 q_2 + \lambda[x^0 - b(q_1, q_2)]$$

which yields

$$\frac{\partial V}{\partial q_1} = p_1 - \lambda b_1 = 0 \qquad\qquad [2.38]$$

$$\frac{\partial V}{\partial q_2} = p_2 - \lambda b_2 = 0 \qquad\qquad [2.39]$$

$$\frac{\partial V}{\partial \lambda} = x^0 - b(q_1, q_2) = 0 \qquad\qquad [2.40]$$

This yields

$$\frac{p_1}{p_2} = \frac{b_1}{b_2} = \text{MRT} \qquad\qquad [2.41]$$

The Lagrangian multiplier λ from [2.38] and [2.39] is given by

$$\lambda = \frac{p_1}{b_1} = \frac{p_2}{b_2} \quad \text{or} \quad \lambda = p_1 \frac{\partial q_1}{\partial x} = p_2 \frac{\partial q_2}{\partial x} \qquad\qquad [2.42]^{10}$$

Thus the VMP of X in the production of each output is equal to λ.

The interpretation of λ might be compared with the interpretation of μ in the cost minimization problem. (See 2.20–2.22.) The total differential of [2.37] is given by

$$dR = p_1 \, dq_1 + p_2 \, dq_2 \qquad\qquad [2.43]$$

If $p_1 = b_1$ and $p_2 = b_2$ are substituted into [2.43] this yields

$$dR = b_1 \, dq_1 + b_2 \, dq_2 \qquad\qquad [2.44]$$

If [2.44] is divided by the total differential of x, [2.35] then

$$\frac{dR}{dx} = \frac{\lambda(b_1 \, dq_1 + b_2 \, dq_2)}{b_1 \, dq_1 + b_2 \, dq_2} = \lambda \qquad\qquad [2.45]$$

which is called the marginal revenue productivity of X. It can be contrasted with μ which is [2.22] which as $\dfrac{dC}{dq}$ is marginal cost of q. X is an input and in this problem the Lagrange multiplier λ is equivalent to its contribution at the margin to revenues, while Q is output and μ is its contribution at the margin to costs.

Notice that the optimality conditions given in [2.41] can be equated at different levels of R and thus form a locus, the *output* expansion path analogous to the expansion path described earlier in the cost minimization problem. Thus in the case of joint production the firm, in solving the revenue maximizing problem, is in an analogous position to the two-input/single-output case. In the latter case, the expansion path gave the input combinations from which the firm would choose, while in the former (joint product) case the output expansion path is giving the *output* combination from which the firm will choose.

Profit maximization

Having established the output combinations from which the firm will choose, it now remains to indicate the conditions for profit maximization with joint products. The profit function is given by:

$$\pi = p_1 q_1 + p_2 q_2 - rh(q_1 q_2)$$

where r = cost of X per unit.

This is maximized as follows:

$$\frac{\partial \pi}{\partial q_1} = p_1 - rh_1 = 0$$

$$\frac{\partial \pi}{\partial q_2} = p_2 - rh_2 = 0$$

These yield $r = \dfrac{p_1}{h_1} = \dfrac{p_2}{h_2}$

which is, substituting from [2.42],

$$r = \frac{p_1 \partial q_1}{\partial x} = \frac{p_2 \partial q_2}{\partial x}$$

Thus VMP of X for the production of each output must be equal to the unit cost of X. It is not very surprising that the unit cost of X is also equal to $\dfrac{dR}{dx}$ (see [2.42] and [2.45]). $\dfrac{dR}{dx}$ is the rate at which an additional unit of X increases the firm's revenue. Clearly it pays to keep on adding units of this until $\dfrac{dR}{dx} = r$.

The multiproduct/multifactor firm

The above analyses of the single-product firm and of the single-factor joint-product firm can be generalized to cover a firm producing m outputs and using n inputs. The production function stated in implicit form is

$$F(q_1, \ldots q_m, x_1, \ldots x_n) = 0 \tag{2.46}$$

This function has the usual properties discussed above: continuous first and second partial derivatives, which are positive for outputs and negative for the inputs.

Profit maximization is achieved in a relatively simple manner by maximizing the profit function, Π, [2.47] subject to the constraint of the production function.

Thus the profit function is

$$\pi = \sum_{i=1}^{m} p_i q_i - \sum_{j=1}^{n} r_j x_j \tag{2.47}$$

Incorporating the production function as a constraint yields the following Lagrangian:

$$W = \sum_{i=1}^{m} p_i q_i - \sum_{j=1}^{n} r_j x_j + \eta F(q_1, \ldots q_m, x_1 \ldots x_n)$$

If each of the $(m + n + 1)$ partial derivatives are equated to zero it follows that

$$\frac{\partial W}{\partial q_i} = p_i + \eta F_i = 0 \qquad i = 1, \ldots, m$$

$$\frac{\partial W}{\partial x_j} = -r_j + \eta F_{m+j} = 0 \qquad j = 1, \ldots, n \tag{2.48}$$

$$\frac{\partial W}{\partial \eta} = F(q_1, \ldots q_m, x_1, \ldots x_n) = 0$$

where $F_i (i = 1 \ldots m + n = s)$ is the partial of [2.46] with respect to its ith argument.

If any two, k and ℓ, of the first m equations in [2.48] are chosen, the ηF_i terms are moved across the equality and one is divided by the other to get rid of η:

$$\frac{p_k}{p_\ell} = \frac{F_k}{F_\ell} = \frac{-\partial q_\ell}{\partial q_k} \qquad k, \ell = 1, \ldots, m.$$

Thus the MRT of every two outputs — holding all other variables constant — is equal to the ratio of their prices. For the kth output and the jth input it follows from [2.48] that

$$\frac{r_j}{p_k} = \frac{-F_{m+j}}{F_k} = \frac{\partial q_k}{\partial x_j} \quad \text{or}$$

$$r_j = p_k \frac{\partial q_k}{\partial x_j} \qquad\qquad \begin{aligned} k &= 1, \ldots, m \\ j &= 1, \ldots, n \end{aligned}$$

which says that VMP of each input with respect to each output is equal to the input price.

Having considered prices and outputs together, and pairs of inputs and outputs together, it only remains to consider inputs together, namely

$$\frac{r_j}{r_p} = \frac{F_{m+j}}{F_{m+p}} = \frac{-\partial x_p}{\partial x_g} \qquad j, p = 1, \ldots, n$$

which simply says that the MRTS for every pair of inputs is equal to the ratio of their prices.

2.6 Comparative statics

The mathematical development of this section is rather specialized. Non-specialists can therefore skim it to get an idea of comparative statics and the firm ignoring the mathematics.

Comparative statics is "the investigation of changes in a system from one position of equilibrium to another without regard to the transitional process involved in the adjustment". (Samuelson, 1947.) Thus taking the system described by equations [2.48] comparative statics is concerned with the measurement of the effects of changes in one variable on the system. In particular it is concerned with the sign relationships. For example, if the price of one factor only increases, does the quantity of it that is used increase or decrease? In the table that concludes this section some sample relationships will therefore be shown by means of signs (+, −). Where the sign relationship is indeterminate this will be indicated by a question mark (?) or the likely sign and a question mark.

Changes in input and output prices
The types of question asked in the comparative static analysis of the firm are: How do changes in the prices of inputs and output affect the

quantities used of these? Such questions can be answered if [2.48] is totally differentiated to give:

$$\eta F_{11}\, dq_1 + \cdots \cdot \eta F_{1(s)}\, dx_n + F_1\, d\eta = -dp_1$$

$$\cdots \cdots \cdots \cdots \cdots \cdots \cdots \cdots \cdots \cdots \qquad [2.49]$$

$$\eta F_{s1}\, dq_1 + \cdots \cdot + \eta F_{ss}\, dx_n + F_s\, d\eta = dr_n$$

$$F_1\, dq_1 + \cdots \cdot + F_s\, dx_n \qquad\qquad = 0$$

On the assumption that price changes are given treating [2.49] as a system of $(s + 1)$ equations and $(s + 1)$ variables $dq_i (i = 1, \ldots, m)$ $dx_j (j = 1, \ldots, n)$ and $d\eta$ and using Cramer's rule to solve for dq_i and dx_j yields

$$dq_i = \frac{-D_{1i}\, dp_1 - \cdots \cdot + D_{si}\, dr_n}{D} \qquad (i = 1 \ldots m)$$

$$dx_j = \frac{-D_{1m+j}\, dp_1 \cdots \cdot + D_{s1m+j}\, dr_n}{D} \qquad (j = 1 \ldots n)$$

where D is the determinant of the coefficients in [2.49], and D_{ij} is the cofactor of the element ij.

The rate of change of quantity with respect to price is derived by dividing both sides of [2.49] by the price differential (dp_i) or (dv_j) and letting the remaining price differentials equal zero:

$$\frac{\partial q_i}{\partial p_\ell} = \frac{\partial q_\ell}{\partial p_i} = \frac{-D_{\ell i}}{D} \qquad i, \ell = 1, \ldots, m \qquad\qquad [2.50]$$

$$\frac{\partial x_j}{\partial r_\ell} = \frac{\partial x_\ell}{\partial r_j} = \frac{D_{m+\ell,\, m+j}}{D} \qquad j, \ell = 1, \ldots, n \qquad\qquad [2.51]$$

$$\frac{\partial q_i}{\partial r_\ell} = \frac{\partial x_\ell}{\partial p_i} = \frac{D_{m+\ell,\, i}}{D} \qquad \begin{array}{l} i = 1, \ldots, m \\ \ell = 1, \ldots, n \end{array} \qquad [2.52]$$

The above results are not obvious. In particular, it is not obvious that in [2.51] the change in the jth factor with respect to a change in the ℓth factor price, output constant, must be equal to the change in the ℓth factor with respect to the jth price. This follows from the fact that the determinant D is symmetric.

Table 2.1   Relationships

| Quantities | Prices | | |
	p_i	p_ϱ	r_ϱ
q_i	+	?	?
x_ϱ	?	?	−

Table 2.1 shows that most of the sign relationships are indeterminate as they depend on the form of the production function. However, the own price effects, e.g., $\dfrac{\partial q_i}{\partial p_i}$ and $\dfrac{\partial x_\varrho}{\partial r_\varrho}$ are unambiguously positive and negative. Thus it is always true that an increase in the ith price other prices constant, will always increase the production of the jth output.

Exercises − 2

1.   Derive an expansion path for the following production functions

(a) $q = A x_1^\alpha x_2^{1-\alpha}$ where $0 < \alpha < 1$

(b) $q = A[\alpha x_1^{-\rho} + (1 - \alpha) x_2^{-\rho}]^{-1/\rho}$

2.   Construct marginal productivity (MP) functions for X_1 and X_2 for the production function $q = x_1 x_2 - 0.1\, x_1^2 - 0.6\, x_2^2$ (When calculating MP of X_1 let $x_2 = 10$ and when calculating MP of X_2 let $x_1 = 20$.)

3.   Have the following production functions convex isoquants? Are the production functions themselves concave (or strictly concave)?

(a) $q = 0.5\, x_1^{0.25} x_2^{0.75}$

(b) $q = x_1 x_2 + x_1 x_3 + x_2 x_3$

4.   Interpret the economic meaning of the Lagrange multiplier, λ in the consumer's problem of maximizing utility subject to a budget constraint, viz.,

Max $L = U(x_1, x_2) - \lambda(p_1 x_1 + p_2 x_2 - M)$

where U = utility functions; x_1, x_2 are commodities, p_1, p_2 are prices, and M = income.

5. Derive the Slutsky equation for the function given in problem 4. Recall that this is derived by total differentiation of the system of equations which results from partial differentiation of L with respect to x_1, x_2, and λ.

6. Calculate elasticity of substitution for the production functions given in Exercise 3.

7. Derive total, marginal, and average cost functions for the production function $q = Ax_1^{\alpha} x_2^{1-\alpha}$ where $\alpha = \frac{1}{2}$, $A = 1$. Assume input prices of $r_1 = 1$ and $r_2 = 1$ and fixed cost of 3.

8. A firm has a short-run total-cost function given by

$$C = q^3 - 8q^2 + 25q + 5$$

Compute:
(a) Output at which profits are maximized if price, $p = 9$.
(b) Output at which MC = AVC.
(c) Value of AVC at MC = AVC.
(d) Output at which AVC is minimized.

9. Construct the envelope of the family of short-run cost-curves in the pq plane given by $p = -3q^2 + qk - k^2$.

10. In elasticity supply at any given moment of time the public utility has a given number of plants each with different (and constant) operating costs. Devise a rule for operating these plants at minimum cost in the short run, and in the long run.

Hint: Demand varies according to time of day and time of year. This implies idleness of plant.

Notes

1. If the axes represent price and quantity continuous functions imply that the variables, in this case price and quantity, are perfectly divisible, or else the functions would have to be represented as "steps" which are discontinuous.

2. A function $f(x)$ is concave if and only if for any two distinct points x^1 and x^2, $\lambda f(x^1) + (1 - \lambda) f(x^2) \leqslant f(\lambda x^1 + (1 - \lambda)x^2)$ and for $0 < \lambda < 1$. The function is strictly concave if the inequality is strict.

3. This is derived by means of the function of a function rule. Let $q = Av^{-1/\rho}$ where $v = [\alpha x_1^{-\rho} + (1 - \alpha)x_2^{-\rho}]$

$$\frac{dq}{dv} = -\frac{Av^{-[(\rho + 1)/\rho]}}{\rho}, \qquad \frac{\partial v}{\partial x_1} = -\rho\alpha x_1^{-(\rho + 1)}$$

$$\frac{\partial q}{\partial x_1} = \frac{\partial q}{\partial v}\frac{\partial v}{\partial x_1} = A\alpha\left[\frac{v^{-1/\rho}}{x_1}\right]^{\rho + 1} = \frac{\alpha}{A^\rho}\left(\frac{q}{x_1}\right)^{\rho + 1}$$

as $q = Av^{-1/\rho}$ and similarly for $\dfrac{\partial q}{\partial x_2}$

For a further and detailed discussion of production functions and alternative means of deriving these results see Heathfield (1971).

4. An alternative derivation is to note that in Fig. 2.3

$$x_1'' = C^{(2)}/r_1 \quad \text{and} \quad x_2'' = C^{(2)}/r_2$$

and that the gradient of $C^{(2)} = -\dfrac{C^{(2)}/r_2}{C^{(2)}/r_1}$

$$= -\frac{r_1}{r_2}$$

5. Maximizing output with a given cost can be demonstrated as follows. Setting up the Lagrangian:

$$\text{Max } L = f(x_1, x_2) + (C^0 - r_1x_1 - r_2x_2)$$

and setting partial derivatives with respect to x_1, x_2 and M equal to zero yields:

$$\frac{\partial L}{\partial x_1} = f_1 - \lambda r_1 = 0$$

$$\frac{\partial L}{\partial x_2} = f_2 - \lambda r_2 = 0$$

$$\frac{\partial V}{\partial \lambda} = C^0 - r_1x_1 - r_2x_2 = 0$$

which yields $\dfrac{f_1}{f_2} = \dfrac{r_1}{r_2} = \text{MRTS}$, which is clearly identical to [2.19].

6. The three expressions are

$$C = K + r_1 x_1 + r_2 x_2$$

$$q = f(x_1, x_2)$$

$$0 = g(x_1 x_2)$$

Recall that the last expression is the expansion path and derived from the minimizing of the cost of a given output. Thus each point on the cost curve is the minimum cost of producing that output.

7. $TC_n - TC_{n-1} = MC = \Delta TC$

More generally let the change in q be Δq and not simply one unit as in [2.26]. Then

$$MC = \frac{\Delta TC}{\Delta q} .$$

Taking the limit of the above expression as $\Delta q \to 0$ it follows that

$$MC = \frac{dTC}{dq}$$

8. This implies some increasing returns indicated by a non-concavity in the production function corresponding to the downward part of the MC curve.

9. The proof is simple.

The procedure is simply to minimize $AVC = \dfrac{\Psi(q)}{q}$,

i.e., $\dfrac{dAVC}{dq} = \dfrac{\Psi'(q)q - \Psi(q)}{q^2} = \dfrac{\Psi'(q)}{q} - \dfrac{\Psi(q)}{q^2} = 0$

which yields $\Psi'(q) = \dfrac{\Psi(q)}{q}$

which is MC = AVC.

10. Recall that $b_1 = \dfrac{\partial x}{\partial q_1}$

Applying the inverse function rule it follows that

$$\frac{1}{b_1} = \frac{\partial q_1}{\partial x} = \text{marginal product of } X.$$

3

Production, cost and equilibrium: programming models

Mathematical programming, like calculus, is a mathematical technique which has considerable significance for economic theory in general, and for the theory of the firm in particular. Linear programming from its very early stages of development was applied in the solution of business and other problems requiring an allocation of scarce resources. For example, it was used in the determination of optimal product lines, in the selection of transportation routes, in the determination of diets meeting certain requirements (this was readily extended to include the problem of making a product to achieve a certain specification), and many other applications. The application of linear programming to such problems of resource allocation was quickly noted by economists interested in the theory of the firm, and led to a re-examination of the neoclassical approach to the firm as outlined in Chapter 2. This exercise resulted in a considerable advance for the theory of the firm, certainly in the direction of making the theory more relevant to problems of the management of real firms. For one thing the linear programming approach does not assume smooth isoquants. For another, unlike the neoclassical analysis, it does not assume that the optimal technical production processes have been worked out. Indeed it will indicate that the optimal combination of production processes is no trivial task. Before such a programming analysis of the theory of the firm can be made it is necessary to examine briefly the nature of programming including the notions of the primal and dual problems. This is done in section 3.1. After this it is possible to re-examine production and cost which are analysed respectively in sections 3.2 and 3.3. Section 3.4, by way of conclusion, makes a comparison between the programming and neoclassical approaches.

3.1 Introduction to programming

Mathematical programming is a set of mathematical techniques concerned with the solution of optimization problems. Unlike the classical calculus methods employed in the analysis of the neoclassical firm mathematical programming is much more general in application and does not, for example, require equality constraints. Mathematical programming as such is entirely a body of mathematical technique. Its interest for the theory of the firm lies in the fact that the "economic" features of problems can be more adequately modelled within a programming framework rather than within the restricted framework of classical calculus. For example, negative quantities of many economic quantities, e.g., goods and factors are quite meaningless. Hence non-negative constraints would appear to be important in the analysis of certain economic problems, including those of the firm. Such issues can be best illustrated by describing a general programming problem.

The general problem of mathematical programming may be stated as the problem of determining the values of n variables $X_1, X_2, \ldots . X_n$ which maximize or minimize the function

$$Z = \Phi(X_1, X_2, \ldots . X_n) \tag{3.1}$$

Subject to m constraints of the form

$$g_i(X_1, X_2, \ldots . X_n) \begin{pmatrix} \leqslant \\ = \\ \geqslant \end{pmatrix} B_i \quad i = 1, 2, \ldots . m \tag{3.2}^1$$

and to the non-negativity constraints

$$X_j \geqslant 0, j = 1, 2, \ldots . n \tag{3.3}$$

Obviously, in [3.2] one and only one of the symbols $\leqslant = \geqslant$ holds for each expression.

Comparison of the programming methods used to solve problem [3.1], [3.2], and [3.3] with the classical calculus optimization methods of neoclassical economics shows that programming methods are more general in at least three ways. Firstly, the non-negativity constraints [3.3] prevent negative values (which are usually nonsensical in economics) but which can quite easily happen with the classical Lagrangian methods employed in Chapter 2. Secondly, the classical calculus methods cannot solve the problem where the objective function and the constraints g_i are all linear — hence the emergence of the linear programming problem which is a special case of [3.1], [3.2] and [3.3]. Thirdly, $g_i(X_1, X_2, \ldots . X_n) \overset{\leqslant}{\underset{\geqslant}{=}} B_i$ for all i, whereas in the classical calculus this could only hold with equality. This feature of classical calculus is highly restrictive in economic terms since it implies that say fixed endowments of certain inputs must all be used up, when they may yield a higher value of the objective function if only some of these are fully used up. These points will become clearer if some simple problems are solved by numerical and graphical methods. These will consist of a simple linear programming problem. These will be followed by a discussion of their economic interpretation including the concept of the dual variables.

Linear programming

An example of a linear programming problem is as follows:

Maximize $z = 6x_1 + 4x_2$

subject to $\quad 2x_1 + 3x_2 \leqslant 12$

$$2x_1 + x_2 \leqslant 8 \qquad\qquad [3.4]$$

$$x_1 \geqslant 0, x_2 \geqslant 0$$

Recalling how it was possible to represent the three variables of a production function, $q = f(x_1, x_2)$, in two-dimensional space through the device of drawing contours corresponding to different levels of q (isoquants) it can easily be seen how it is possible to derive analogous contours representing levels of Z. In this case, however, they would be straight lines.

Fig. 3.1

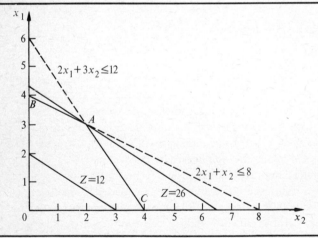

Two such contours are drawn for purposes of illustration in Fig. 3.1. Using the same approach as in Chapter 2 which implies getting onto the highest contour it is clear that the contour $z = 26$, as drawn, is a maximum, as this is the highest contour which just touches the feasible area. Thus $x_1 = 3$, and $x_2 = 2$ represents the solution to this problem, since these are the only values of x_1 and x_2 consistent with both $Z = 26$ and the constraints.

The above problem is known as the *primal problem*. The *dual* of this is constructed by substituting "minimize", and substituting $\geqslant$ for $\leqslant$, and rearranging rows and columns. In terms [3.4] this means that 12 and 8 on the right-hand side of the constraints are interchanged with the coefficient 6 and 4 variables are renamed y_1 and y_2. Thus the dual is

Minimize $x = 12y_1 + 8y_2$

subject to $\qquad 2y_1 + 2y_2 \geqslant 6$

$\qquad\qquad\quad 3y_1 + \ y_2 \geqslant 4$ $\qquad\qquad\qquad\qquad\qquad$ [3.5]

$\qquad\qquad\quad y_1 \geqslant 0, y_2 \geqslant 0$

The solution of this problem turns out to be $y_1 = \frac{1}{2}$, and $y_2 = 2\frac{1}{2}$. (The reader is invited to check this in Exercise 1 at the end of this chapter.) The important result is that at these values $x = 26 = z$ which is a fundamental result in linear programming, known as the *duality theorem*[2]. The economic implications of duality are of considerable significance, as is explained later in the chapter. However, before discussing them by way of examples it will prove useful to examine non-linear programming.

Non-linear programming and the Kuhn-Tucker conditions
The Kuhn-Tucker conditions represent the most powerful approach to the solution of non-linear programming problems. For illustrative purposes (and entirely without proofs) the Kuhn-Tucker conditions will be set out for the problem [3.1], [3.2], and [3.3], for the case where [3.1] is to be maximized.

Thus the problem is to

Maximize $Z = \Phi(X_1, X_2, \ldots . X_n)$

subject to $\qquad g_i(X_1, X_2, \ldots . X_n) \leqslant B_i$

$\qquad\qquad\quad X_j \geqslant 0, \quad j = 1, \ldots . n, \quad i = 1, \ldots . m.$

The first step is to form the Lagrangian:

$$L = Z + \sum_{i=1}^{m} \lambda_i(B_i - g_i) \, x_1, x_2, \ldots . x_n \geqslant 0, \quad \lambda_1, \ldots . \lambda_m \geqslant 0 \quad [3.6]$$

Finding an optimum value of this function requires that L be maximized with respect to the variables X_j and minimized with respect to the

Lagrange multipliers λ_i. The Kuhn-Tucker conditions may be written as follows:

$$\frac{\partial L}{\partial x_j} \leqslant 0; \quad x_j \frac{\partial L}{\partial x_j} = 0; \quad x_j \geqslant 0, \quad j = 1, \dots n \qquad [3.7]$$

$$\frac{\partial L}{\partial \lambda_i} \geqslant 0; \quad \lambda_i \frac{\partial L}{\partial \lambda_i} = 0; \quad \lambda_i \geqslant 0, \quad i = 1, \dots m \qquad [3.8]$$

The differences between [3.7] and [3.8] and the optimum conditions using classical calculus arise from the fact that the values of the variables are constrained to the positive quadrant[3].

The application of the Kuhn-Tucker conditions can be illustrated in the following simple example (which will be given economic significance later).

Maximize $Z = 11x_1 - x_1^2 + 7x_2 - 2x_2^2 - 3y$ $\qquad [3.9]$

subject to $\qquad x_1 \leqslant y$ $\qquad [3.10]$

$\qquad\qquad\qquad x_2 \leqslant y$ $\qquad [3.11]$

Form the Lagrangian and set out Kuhn-Tucker conditions:

$$L = 11x_1 - x_1^2 + 7x_2 - 2x_2^2 - 3y + \lambda_1(y - x_1) + \lambda_2(y - x_2) \qquad [3.12]$$

$$\frac{\partial L}{\partial x_1} = 11 - 2x_1 - \lambda_1 \leqslant 0; \quad x_1(11 - 2x_1 - \lambda_1) = 0; \quad x_1 \geqslant 0 \qquad [3.13]$$

$$\frac{\partial L}{\partial x_2} = 7 - 4x_2 - \lambda_2 \leqslant 0; \quad x_2(7 - 4x_2 - \lambda_2) = 0; \quad x_2 \geqslant 0 \qquad [3.14]$$

$$\frac{\partial L}{\partial y} = -3 + \lambda_1 + \lambda_2 \leqslant 0; \quad y(-3 + \lambda_1 + \lambda_2) = 0; \quad y \geqslant 0 \qquad [3.15]$$

$$\frac{\partial L}{\partial \lambda_1} = y - x_1 \geqslant 0; \quad \lambda_1(y - x_1) = 0; \quad \lambda_1 \geqslant 0 \qquad [3.16]$$

$$\frac{\partial L}{\partial \lambda_2} = y - x_2 \geqslant 0; \quad \lambda_2(y - x_2) = 0; \quad \lambda_2 \geqslant 0 \qquad [3.17]$$

Notice that the Kuhn-Tucker conditions while characterizing a solution do not actually provide a method of obtaining a solution. Thus various combinations of x_1, x_2, λ_1 and λ_2 can be devised, e.g.:

$$x_1 = 0, \quad x_2 = 0, \quad y = 0, \quad \lambda_1 = 0, \quad \lambda_2 = 0 \qquad [1]$$

$$x_1 > 0, \quad x_2 = 0, \quad y > 0, \quad \lambda_1 > 0, \quad \lambda_2 = 0 \qquad [2]$$

$$x_1 = 0, \quad x_2 > 0, \quad y > 0, \quad \lambda_1 = 0, \quad \lambda_2 > 0 \qquad [3]$$

$$x_1 > 0, \quad x_2 > 0, \quad y > 0, \quad \lambda_1 > 0, \quad \lambda_2 > 0 \qquad [4]$$

$$x_1 > 0, \quad x_2 > 0, \quad y > 0, \quad \lambda_1 > 0, \quad \lambda_2 = 0 \qquad [5]$$

The maximum profit solution is given by [5] as follows:

$$x_1 = 4, x_2 = 7/4, y = 4, \lambda_1 = 3, Z = 22\tfrac{1}{8}$$

The reader should verify this for himself by working through the rest of the possible combinations, using the Kuhn-Tucker conditions that [5] is in fact the only optimal solution. (Sec Exercise 2 at the end of this chapter.)

Economic interpretation of dual variables
To illustrate the economic significance of duality it is necessary to go back to [3.4] which corresponds to the mathematical formulation of the following problem faced by a firm.

A firm produces two products X_1 and X_2. The profits per unit of output from these products are 6 and 4 respectively. Each product needs to be worked on two machines. The firm has 12 machine hours available on machine 1 and 8 machine hours available on machine 2. X_1 requires 2 hours of both machine 1 and 2 per unit produced and X_2 3 hours of machine 1 and 1 hour of machine 2. The solution of [3.4] $x_1 = 3, x_2 = 2$ given therefore the amounts of X_1 and X_2 that the firm should produce in order to maximize profits.

Similarly the non-linear programming problem presented in [3.8], [3.9], and [3.10] can be represented as a simple peak-load problem. In this case the firm is a monopolist[4] with demands that vary in the course of a day, the effect of which is to create one period when its capacity is fully-utilized and another period when demand is slow so that capacity is under-utilized. Demand in the peak period is represented by the linear expression $11 - x_1$ while in the off-peak period it is $7 - 2x_2$. Capacity costs are 3 per unit per period. Thus the expression [3.9] is interpreted as the profit function, that is TR − TC, while [3.10] and [3.11] are the capacity constraints.

Recall that the optimal (profit maximizing) solution was $x_1 = 4$, $x_2 = 7/4$, $y = 4$ and $\lambda_1 = 3$. The meaning of x_1, x_2, and y are respectively the amounts sold in periods 1 and 2 and the amount of capacity which maximize profit. The meaning of λ_1 is less obvious. In fact it is marginal revenue in period 1. It is also known as one of the dual variables, the other one being λ_2. This, and other economic aspects of duality will now be examined.

In Chapter 2 (p. 22) a Lagrangian multiplier was interpreted as marginal cost. Generally the ith dual variable will be shown to represent the (marginal) effect on the objective function of relaxing the ith constraint. This will be shown in both the linear and non-linear programming cases. The meaning of the dual variables in the linear case can be simply demonstrated with the aid of two theorems: the duality theorem (p. 47 and note 2) and another theorem, which will be discussed below, called the basis theorem[5]. Before doing this it is necessary to note that a solution to a linear problem will occur at any corner of the feasible region. Thus in terms of Fig. 3.1 points A, B, C, and 0 form a basic solution. (See Baumol, 1972, pp. 82–4.) In this case A is seen to be the optimal point. If either constraint is relaxed, e.g., if the first constraint became 13 instead of 12 the constraint line can be seen to move outward but retain the same slope. A similar parallel shift could take place for the other constraint. The basis theorem is relevant in such cases and may be interpreted as implying that if one or more of the constraints are varied in parallel fashion and a particular extreme part, in this case A, is optimal, the equivalent extreme point A^1 will be optimal following the variation of the constraints described above.

This can be considered in the case of problems like [3.4] which may be written in general as

Maximize px

subject to $ax \leqslant b$

$$x \geqslant 0$$

In line with the above description of the basis theorem the primal constraint vector b is changed to $b + \Delta b$, subject, of course, to the condition that the original basis A remains feasible. The variation in the optimal value of objective function Z^* is given by

$\Delta Z^* = y^* \, \Delta b$ (by duality theorem)

If x^*, x' are optimal vectors in the original and varied cases it follows that as the original basis remains feasible, y^* will remain the optimal dual vector. Thus

$px' = y^*(b + \Delta b)$

$px^* = y^* \, b$

and by subtraction $px' - px^* = \Delta Z^* = y^* \, \Delta b$ [3.18]

The interpretation of the dual variables can readily be derived from [3.17]. If it is assumed that only the ith constraint varies then

$$\frac{\Delta Z^*}{b_i} = y_i^* \qquad [3.19]$$

which interprets the ith dual variable as the marginal effect on the objective function arising from the relaxation of the ith constraint.

Exactly the same interpretation applies to the Lagrangian multipliers in [3.11] which are also called the dual variables[6]. The economic interpretation can now readily be made of the dual variables in problems [3.5] and [3.8]. The y_i in problem [3.5] may be defined as the effect on the objective function (profit) of relaxing the ith constraint (types of machine). *Thus the y_i gives the marginal value to the firm of the ith resource.* Thus the dual problem requires that the *minimum* value for each of the firm's fixed inputs be found which completely accounts for all of the profits of each of its outputs. This has an interesting implication regarding decision making procedures within the firm. Top management of a firm may thus issue dual prices y_i to plant managers of each input. The managers are then in a position to produce which product line they feel is appropriate. If a manager produces non-optimal quantities of the products concerned he will incur a loss. If his decisions, however, are optimal he will just break even, as these dual accounting prices are designed to exhaust exactly the profit. In terms of the simplified example [3.4], the plant manager would buy 12 units of machine 1 time and 8 units of machine 2 time. These would "cost" him 26. Only by producing 3 of x_1 and 2 of x_2 would he be able to just break even at selling prices of 6 and 4. Thus linear programming has already even in this simple form indicated how a firm might adopt a policy of decentralized decision making. As such it is relating to the nature of real firms in a way not done by one neoclassical theory of the firm which is silent on such problems. Such considerations will be further examined in Chapter 5.

As mentioned briefly above, the λ_i in the non-linear programming problem [3.8] are marginal revenues. This follows directly from the definition of a Lagrange multiplier. λ_i represents the marginal effect on net revenue of relaxing the capacity constraint. This can be noted from, e.g., expression [3.13] where $\lambda_1 = 11 - 2x_1$, which is clearly marginal revenue or the change in total revenue from selling one more unit[7].

3.2 Linear programming and the theory of production

The analysis of section 3.1 stands in contrast to most of Chapter 2 in that it examines the multiproduct firm (using the simplest example of two products). While the multiproduct firm is both more realistic and more general than the single-product firm the approach outlined suffers from a number of limitations; the most important being that each output is restricted to a single production process. Each product requires inputs in a fixed ratio and therefore cannot use up excess amounts of any input. In view of the emphasis placed upon substitutability in economics it will now be shown how substitution between inputs can take place within the linear programming context. To achieve this and to facilitate comparison with the neoclassical firm of Chapter 2 it will be necessary to return to examination of the single-product firm.

An illustrative numerical example
The linear programming problem takes slightly different form from the example given in [3.5]. The problem is

Maximize profits $= Z = 0.75x_1 + 0.9x_2 + 1.0x_3 + 1.2x_4$		[3.23]
Subject to	$4x_1 + 5x_2 + 6x_3 + 8x_4 \leqslant 500$	[3.24]
	$7x_1 + 6x_2 + 5x_3 + 4x_4 \leqslant 800$	[3.25]

The variables X_1, X_2, X_3, and X_4 have different meaning from the earlier example. X_1, X_2, X_3, and X_4 are the *same* product. The variables simply represent quantities produced by different processes. This will be clear from the description of the problem given below:

The firm produces a single product of which it can sell as much as it wishes at 4 per unit. Two types of machine are required to produce the product. The firm has 500 hours available of machine 1 and 800 of machine 2 per period. It can produce the product only by using machines 1 and 2. Each column in [3.24] and [3.25] can therefore be seen as a process, since it represents the combination of inputs required to produce output. Thus process 1 is relatively economical in the use of machine 1 while process 4 is relatively economical in the use of machine 2. The coefficients of the profit function are derived by taking the price of the product and deducting the variable costs per unit (AVC) associated with each process, namely 3.25, 3.1, 3.0, and 2.8. For example more labour and materials are used in process 1 than in the other processes with the effect that the profit per unit is greater in the other processes as shown in [3.23].

These features can all be combined in a diagram to show how equilibrium of the firm is achieved. This is done in Fig. 3.2. Each process is shown and identified by its number. Process 1 is relatively economical in its use of machine 1 while process 4 is relatively economical in its use of machine 2.

The process rays can be easily constructed by plotting in the case of process 1, the coefficients 4 and 7 on the machine 1 and machine 2 axes respectively. These coefficients mean that whatever the output of the commodity produced by process X that machine 1 and machine 2 will always be used in the proportions of 4 to 7. Thus process 1 can be represented by the ray, P_1, and the other processes by rays P_2, P_3, and P_4.

Fig. 3.2

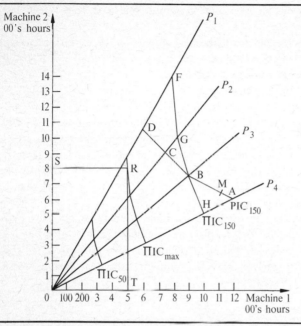

From the processes shown in Fig. 3.2 it is possible to derive production indifference curves (isoquants) and profit indifference curves corresponding to output of 150 is shown as PIC$_{150}$ and as ABCD. The construction of this is obtained by multiplying, in the case of P_4, the output by 8 and 4 (because process 4 uses 8 hours of machine 1 and 4 hours of machine 2 to produce one unit of output). This gives the point 1200 hours of machine 1 and 600 hours of machine 2. The other points B, C, and D are derived in a similar manner. The rationale of joining points ABCD to form PIC$_{150}$ arises from the fact that a straight line between points A and B represents combinations of P_1 and P_2. In particular the midpoint of AB would represent the production of 75 units from each process. Similarly if a point M is taken which is $\frac{3}{4}$ of the way from B towards A this implies that $\frac{1}{4}$ of P_3 and $\frac{3}{4}$ of P_4 are used, namely 37.5 from P_3 and 112.5 from P_4.

Profit indifference curves (Π IC's) can also be derived. For example, in Fig. 3.2 a profit indifference curve for a profit of 150, is derived and shown as by Π IC_{150} or FGBH, which is simply the locus of points giving a profit of 150. It is clear that a profit of 150 can be provided from P_3 by an output of 150 since the profit in this process is 1 per unit. Thus point B is common to profit and production indifference curves of 150. Output produced by process 4 results in a profit of 1.2 per unit thus the point H can be derived corresponding to an output of 125 using process 4. Similarly, points G and F correspond to outputs of 166.7 from P_2 and 200 from P_1.

To determine maximum profit the next step would be to derive a profit indifference map, which would just be a set of curves like Π IC_{150} all parallel to one another. Profits would be maximized by the firm attaining the highest profit indifference curve. It is of course restricted in this respect by the constraints which it faces. These are given by RS and RT, which correspond to the limits respectively of 800 on machine 1 and 500 on machine 2. From Fig. 3.2 it can readily be seen that the highest profit indifference curve satisfies these constraints at point R. This actually corresponds to a profit of 92.73[8]. Intuitively this can be noted from the diagram by noting that the Π IC max curve is rather closer to the Π IC_{50} curve than it is to the Π IC_{150} curve.

The above procedure clearly has something in common with the neoclassical theory of production. (This will be examined in section 3.3.) It will be necessary, however, first to derive a marginal cost curve for this case so that the comparison may be complete. Marginal cost is a step function as shown in Fig. 3.3.

Fig. 3.3

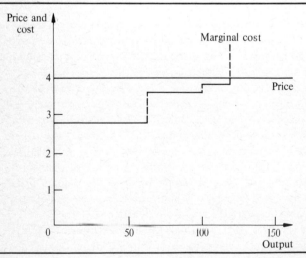

As process 4 happens to be the "cheapest" process, having the lowest variable cost of 2.8 (selling price, 4 less profit per unit 1.2), it is used first. However, it is possible only to produce 62.5 using this process (machine 1 becomes fully employed at this output). With a price (MR = AR) of 4 it clearly pays to produce more than this as long as marginal cost is less than 4. This can be noted in Fig. 3.3. Marginal cost is calculated by starting from the variable costs of each process. When output of 62.5 is reached the only way output can be expanded is by bringing process 3 into operation. This uses 6 units of machine 1 against the 8 used by process 4. Thus $1\frac{1}{3}$ units can be produced by process 3 at the expense of 1 unit foregone produced by process 4. The extra cost of this is as follows:

$$1\tfrac{1}{3} \cdot VC_3 - VC_4 = 1\tfrac{1}{3} \cdot 3 - 2.8 = 1.2$$

which represents the marginal cost of $\frac{1}{3}$ of a unit. Thus if this is multiplied by 3 MC_3 is arrived at:

$$MC_3 = 3.6$$

MC_2 can similarly be derived at 3.6, as can MC_1 at 3.85[9].

Notice how marginal cost rises in discontinuous jumps as capacity of each process is reached until finally maximum output of 118.18 is achieved.

3.3 Comparison of programming and neoclassical approaches

Following the examination of the programming and neoclassical approaches to the theory of the firm, developed in this chapter and in Chapter 2, it seems appropriate at this stage to make a comparison between the two approaches.

The firm, as discussed, might be regarded as having two problems. The first of these consists of finding a method of achieving a physical maximization of output; the second problem is that of maximizing profit. These two problems must either be solved in the above order or be solved simultaneously. The neoclassical theory solves them in order. In particular, in assuming a production function, it assumes that a physical maximization of output for given levels of input has been achieved. This enables it to proceed to the second problem, of maximizing profit subject to the conditions imposed by the production problem. This amounts merely to choosing a level of output which maximizes profit.

By contrast, the linear programming approach solves both problems simultaneously. This is apparent from sections 3.1 and 3.2 of this chapter where the linear programming determined both the optimal quantities of output to be produced and the optimal ways of doing this. Linear programming is more relevant to the problems of real firms because the nature of their problems is such that they are not amenable to solution along the lines of the neoclassical firm. In particular, it will usually be quite pointless to try to derive a (continuous and differentiable) production function, as a function with such properties may not exist. Linear programming, on the other hand, is ideally suited to dealing with the kinds of discontinuities, finite number of techniques, and so on, faced by firms. Linear programming has therefore become a major tool for solving a wide range of problems within firms[10].

Exercises — 3

1. Check that the optimal values of the linear programming dual of [3.5] are $y_1 = \frac{1}{2}$, and $y_2 = 2\frac{1}{2}$. Show that at the optimum $x = 26$.

2. Show that the values of Z implied by Kuhn-Tucker conditions [1], [2], and [3] are less than [4] or [5]. Can you think of any possibilities other than the five given? Do they satisfy the K-T conditions?

3. Verify that the problem given by [3.22], [3.23], and [3.24] is maximized for $x_1 = 90.91$ and $x_2 = 27.27$ with $z = 92.7$.

Hint: Draw a diagram of your own similar to Fig. 3.1.

4. Derive MC_2 and MC_1 for problems [3.22], [3.23], and [3.24].

5. A public utility faces two demands given by $P_1 = 50 - x_1$ in the peak period (period 1) and $P_2 = 30 - 2x_2$ in period 2. It can supply output from either plant 1 or plant 2. Plant 1 has capacity costs of 6 per unit and plant 2, 3 per unit. Running costs are 1 and 3 respectively per unit. Determine optimal prices, P_1 and P_2; optimal quantities of capacity $\bar{q}_1, \bar{q}_2$; optimal outputs x_1, x_2; optimal quantities supplied by each plant $q_{11}, q_{12}, q_{21}, q_{22}$ where the first subscript identifies the plant and the second the period.

Hint: $Q = (q_{11}, q_{21}, q_{12}, q_{22}, \bar{q}_1, \bar{q}_2)$ is given by $Q^0 = (x_2, x_1 - x_2, x_2, 0, x_2, x_1 - x_2)$. Derive K-T conditions.

Notes

1. The reader will recall that [3.2] may be written out in full as

$$g_1(x_1, x_2, \ldots . x_n) \leqslant b_1$$
$$g_2(x_1, x_2, \ldots . x_n) \leqslant b_2$$

. .

. .

. .

$$g_m(x_1, x_2, \ldots . x_n) \leqslant b_m$$

2. The reader interested in proofs of this and other results in linear programming should consult Baumol (1972) for a simple but relatively comprehensive treatment, and Hadley (1964) for a more technical approach.

3. A very simple relationale, which might be helpful to some readers is given below with the aid of a diagram which illustrates the problem of maximizing Z.

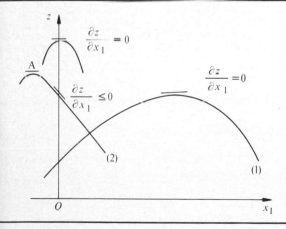

Where the values of x_1 are constrained to being non-negative three situations can occur. The first of these is the familiar one shown as (1) in the diagram where $\dfrac{\partial Z}{\partial x_1} = 0$ and x_1 is positive.

The Kuhn-Tucker conditions deal with this case as can be seen from [3.7]. They also handle case (2). In this case the direct application of classical calculus would lead to point A, but this would violate the non-negativity constraint x, $z \geqslant 0$. From the diagram it can be seen that z is maximized where

$$x_1 = 0 \quad \text{and} \quad \frac{\partial Z}{\partial x_1} < 0.$$

Examination of the Kuhn-Tucker conditions reveals that this eventuality is included. Similarly the other possibility of Z actually reaching its maximum at $x_1 = 0$, shown as case (3) on the diagram, is also included in the Kuhn-Tucker conditions. The reader wishing to pursue this in more detail should consult Hadley (1964).

4.   The monopolist in neoclassical economics is examined in Chapter 4. Readers not completely familiar with this concept in elementary economics should consult pp. 68—71 before proceeding with this example.

5.   This theorem was developed by Gale (1960) and demonstrated by Lancaster (1968).

6.   The detailed proofs may be found in Hadley (1964), pp. 72—5.

$$\frac{\partial Z^*}{\partial b_i} = \sum_{j=1}^{n} \frac{\partial \Phi}{\partial x_j^*} \frac{\partial x_j}{\partial b_i} \quad \text{[3.20] (function of a function rule)}$$

$$\sum_{j=1}^{n} \frac{\partial g_k}{\partial x_j^*} \cdot \frac{\partial x_j^*}{\partial b_i} \quad \begin{array}{l} = 1 \text{ where } i = k \\ = 0 \text{ where } i \neq k \end{array}$$

This can be written as

$$\delta_{ik} - \sum_{j=1}^{n} \frac{\partial g_k}{\partial x_j^*} \frac{\partial x_j^*}{\partial b_i} = 0 \quad \text{[3.21] where } \delta_{ik} \text{ is Kronecker delta.}$$
$$i, k = 1 \ldots . m$$

If [3.21] is multiplied by λ_k^*, summed over k and added to [3.20] this yields

$$\frac{\partial Z^*}{\partial b_i} = \sum_{k=1}^{m} \lambda_k^* \delta_{ik} + \sum_{j=1}^{n} \left[\frac{\partial \Phi}{\partial x_j^*} - \sum_{k=1}^{m} \lambda_k^* \frac{\partial g_k}{\partial x_j^*} \right] \frac{\partial x_j^*}{\partial b_i} \quad \text{[3.22]}$$

The bracketed expression in [3.22] is equal to zero. (This may be checked by examining the first order conditions for an optimum of any Lagrangian problem. Thus

$$\frac{\partial Z^*}{\partial b_i} = \lambda_i^* .)$$

7.   For a more detailed explanation and justification of this see Crew and Kleindorfer (1971).

8.   The reader is encouraged to derive this result using the conventional linear programming approach as Exercise 3 at the end of this chapter.

9.   The reader is encouraged to calculate these for himself as Exercise 4 at the end of this chapter.

10. The range is considerable, including many resource allocation problems, and location problems. Such operations research methods are beyond the scope of this book but may be examined in books like Hadley (1962), and Charnes and Cooper (1961).

4

Market organization: neoclassical approach

The first three chapters of this book have been mainly concerned with aspects of the internal organization of the firm. The production and cost aspects of the firm have been to the fore. The environment in which the firm operates, the markets in which it sells its products, have been virtually ignored. In order to show the nature of the equilibrium of the firm some very simple assumptions — e.g., such as that the firm could sell all it wanted at a price over which it has no control — have been made. Apart from this, however, nothing has been said about the revenue side of the firm's activities. This chapter will examine in detail the revenue side, and bring it together with the cost side discussed above. It will show how different market situations affect not only individual firm behaviour but also how resources are allocated between firms and consumers.

Two assumptions at the heart of the neoclassical approach are worth stressing. Firstly, a "free" market is assumed in the sense that there is no governmental interference at all in its operation. This obviously differs considerably from reality and the issue will be re-assessed in Chapter 7. Secondly, profit maximization is again assumed throughout this chapter, although certain parts, which deal with oligopoly, will show how tenuous the assumption starts to become in the indeterminate situations which occur under collusion and limit pricing. Later chapters again will be concerned with the effects of its relaxation.

The analysis which is set out in this chapter has formed the theoretical basis of much of the branch of applied economics known as industrial organization. This theory has been applied to problems of public policy. Thus it is fairly common in textbooks, when describing models of markets, to discuss policy implications of these models. However, this chapter refrains from discussion of policy implications at this stage, deferring it until Chapter 7 where such public policy issues are discussed within a much wider context.

There are two polar cases of market forms which have been the subject of much analysis in economics from the earliest times. There are *perfect competition* and *monopoly*. Both are concerned with the sale of a homogeneous product. The former has many sellers of the product, while the latter has one seller. All other market forms fall between these two. Oligopoly, for example, may involve the sale of a homogeneous product by a few sellers. Monopolistic competition involves the sale by many sellers of so-called differentiated products. These market situations will now be described in detail.

4.1 Perfect competition

Perfect competition is defined by four important assumptions:

1. Large numbers of firms and consumers, all of small size.

2. Homogeneous product.

3. Free mobility of resources.

4. Perfect knowledge.

These are all to some extent self-explanatory, but some further detailed comment may prove useful.

1. This assumption requires that there is a large number of firms and consumers. This means that each consumer is so small that he cannot gain special consideration from the sellers. Similarly, each firm is so small as to be unable to affect market price by altering its output.

2. A unit of product is identical for each and every seller.

3. Resources can readily move into the market in response to certain signals, principally profits. This implies that labour is mobile between jobs and that new firms and capital may enter the industry without great difficulty.

4. Consumers, factor owners, and firms must possess perfect knowledge if the market is to be competitive. For example if consumers were not perfectly knowledgeable about prices they might pay higher prices when lower ones were available.

With these assumptions the equilibrium of the firm and the industry (which is defined as a collection of firms producing a homogeneous product) is usually derived for the short run, for the long run, and sometimes for the market period. These three kinds of equilibrium will now be examined.

Equilibrium in the market period
Previously the short run and the long run have been discussed. The market period is not covered by the short or the long run since the market period is defined as that period during which output cannot be varied. This occurs for example immediately after a harvest, or when fishing boats have unloaded their catch. In the market period each firm has a fixed quantity to sell and so there is no point in studying its behaviour since by definition it cannot vary its output which it just sells off at the market price.

Fig. 4.1

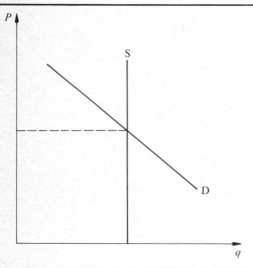

Industry equilibrium is, however, worth examining. Industry supply is determined by taking the horizontal sum of the individual firm's supply curves as shown in Fig. 4.1. This is simply a vertical straight line, since in the market period each firm's supply cannot be altered. Market equilibrium is attained at that point which exactly clears the market at *P* in Fig. 4.1. If demand were less (more) prices would be less (more).

Short run equilibrium
As the individual firm has to accept the price because it is too small to affect price by altering its output its problem becomes that of adjusting its output so as to maximize profits. In particular, as noted in section 2.4, it aims to

maximize $\pi = \text{TR} - \text{TC}$

which, since $TR = p \cdot q$, simply involves equating price with marginal cost, which is the fundamental behavioural rule for the firm in perfect competition.

In the short run the firm, by adopting the $p = MC$ rule, may make profits, or break-even, or incur losses, or cease to produce. The latter case would occur where price is less than average variable costs, as shown in

Fig. 4.2

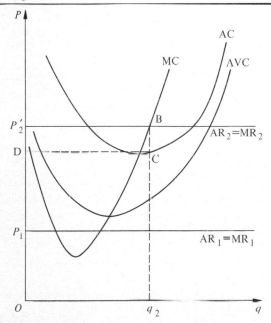

Fig. 4.2 by horizontal line $P_1 = AR_1 = MR_1$. By contrast $P_2 = AR_2 = MR_2$ at output q_2^* and yields a profit of $P_2'BCD$ in the short run.

Equilibrium of the industry in the short run occurs where supply and demand intersect in the familiar manner as shown in Fig. 4.3a. It should be noted in passing that the industry supply curve in the short run is not necessarily the sum of the relevant portion of the marginal cost curves for each producer, since if the industry expands this is likely to push up input prices and therefore shift individual marginal cost curves. In Fig. 4.3a the price is determined at P^* and industry output at Q^*.

In Fig. 4.3b the firm's position is illustrated. If its costs were AC_1, MC_1 it would produce Q_1 and make a profit. If they were AC_2, MC_2 it would produce Q_2 and make a loss.

Fig. 4.3

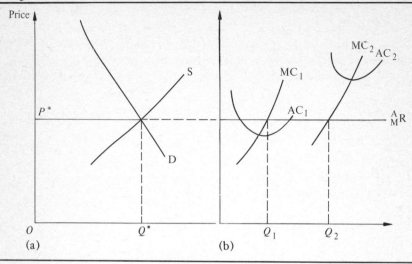

(a)   (b)

Long run adjustment and equilibrium

It is clear from the above analysis of short run equilibrium that the firm in the short run is simply a quantity adjuster. It accepts price and merely adjusts quantity produced to maximize profit. This is all it can do (apart from closing down, which is an extreme form of quantity adjustment). In the long run, however, several alternatives are available. Established firms might leave the industry, or reduce their capacity or increase their

Fig. 4.4

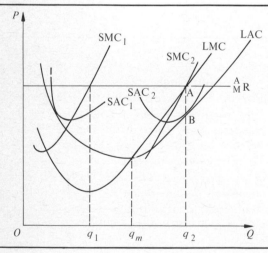

capacity. New firms might enter the industry. What happens depends upon profits. Profits are the signal for expansion or entry. Conversely losses are the signal for contraction or exit. All these can occur in the long run.

The individual firm's adjustment to the signal provided by profits is now illustrated. In Fig. 4.4 the firm is making profits in the short run by an output of q_1 at the market given price of p. Since at q_1 the firm is not on its LAC curve, it is more profitable for the firm to expand its output (and capacity) so that it is on the LAC at output q_2. This point of course does not correspond to the minimum of costs which is given at output of q_m. The reason why this occurs will be given below after discussion of the long run adjustment of the industry.

What happens to the industry depends on the state of the individual firms. If all the other firms but the one described above were producing q_1 on SAC_1 then the adjustment of the above firm would by definition have no effect on the others, and all firms would earn a (temporary) profit of AB per unit. New firms would be attracted by these profits and would enter the industry. This is part of the process of long run adjustment leading to long run equilibrium which is now described with the aid of Figs. 4.5a and 4.5b.

The presence of profits AB per unit attracts other firms to the industry which shifts the supply curve from S_1 to S_2 in Fig. 4.5a; quantity supplied

Fig. 4.5

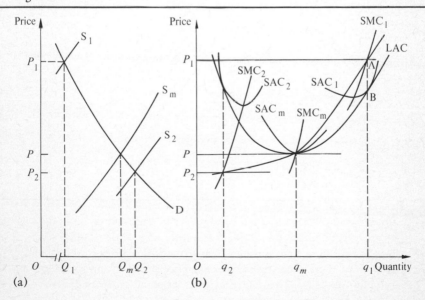

(a)   (b)

by the industry to OQ_2, and price to P_2. The effect of this is for firms to incur losses. Even firms that can quickly adjust to "optimal" plant size[1] of SAC_2 incur losses.

The effect of these losses is for firms to contract the size of their operations or get out of the industry until long run equilibrium is achieved at $SAC_M = SMC_M$ for the firm, and at P and Qm for the industry and P and qm for the firm. This is long run equilibrium and represents the minimum of average costs. This position is clearly equilibrium because there is no incentive for firms to leave the industry or for new firms to enter the industry.

Constant cost and increasing cost industries

An implicit assumption of the analysis of adjustment and equilibrium described above is that the industry was one of "constant costs" in the sense that expanded use of resources did not bid up input prices. Thus in addition to perfect competition in the product market it was implicitly assumed that there was perfect competition in the input market. This can

Fig. 4.6

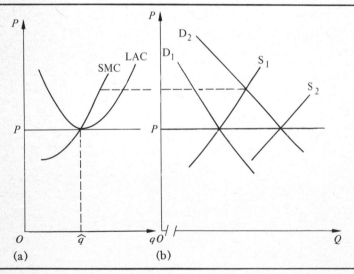

(a)   (b)

be illustrated by means of Figs. 4.6a and 4.6b. Figure 4.6a shows the firm in long run equilibrium producing $\hat{q}$ at a price of p. If demand is increased to D_2 the firm now earns profits which attract other firms to the industry. The entry of these other firms does not raise prices of inputs. Thus long run equilibrium is finally attained at price of p and quantity of $\hat{q}$ for each firm, but with an increased number of firms.

An extreme form of constant cost industries occurs where the firms in the industry display constant returns to scale. This results in what Samuelson has called "indeterminacy in purest competition". As the firm in this case faces constant unit costs and a horizontal demand curve, only three possibilities exist: price is always greater than marginal cost, thus inducing the firm to expand indefinitely; price is less than marginal cost, thus no output will be produced; price is equal to marginal cost, which is consistent with any level of output whatsoever. However, although the output of every firm may be indeterminate the sum of their outputs may be determinate. Thus if several firms expand, others must contract. This does not mean that one firm can grow and grow until it corners the market. Because the firm's demand curve is horizontal and because the long run supply curve of competitors is horizontal even if it produces all the output, it cannot restrict output so as to gain monopoly profit or anything at all. (Any attempt to raise price means that it sells nothing, and other firms flood in to the market which has free entry.)

Fig. 4.7

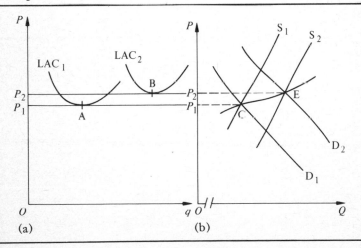

(a)　　　　　　　　　　(b)

Increasing cost industries occur where an expansion of the industry pushes up the prices of inputs. This is shown in Figs. 4.7a and 4.7b. The effect on the firm of a shift in demand from D_1 to D_2 in Fig. 4.7b is shown in Fig. 4.7a.

The firm is originally operating in long run equilibrium at A. It makes a temporary profit as a result of the increase in demand to D_2. This attracts firms to the industry which pushes up the price of inputs to all firms, which shifts the cost curves upward until finally equilibrium for the firm is achieved at B on LAC₂. Notice that the supply curve has also shifted to the right but, because of the increase in price, by not as much as in the constant cost case. The number of firms in the industry as well as output of the industry has increased. The output of the firm in the case illustrated has increased. However, this cannot be predicted. (It may increase, decrease or stay the same.)

4.2 Pure monopoly

Pure monopoly, like perfect competition, is a polar case, whose exacting conditions never exist in the real world. Many markets, however, closely approximate monopoly organization. Pure monopoly is said to exist if there is one and only one seller in a well defined market. Monopoly may arise from a number of sources: patents, control of raw materials, the so-called "natural" monopoly[2] and franchises are some common sources. Devices like these may be grouped together under the general heading of barriers to entry. As will be noted below, these restraints on entry are so important in that they effectively mask the signal provided by profits in the competitive model.

Fig. 4.8

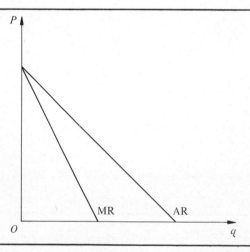

Because the monopoly is the only firm supplying the market (which consists of many consumers) the monopolist's demand curve unlike that of the firm in perfect competition is the market demand curve. This is shown as average revenue (AR) along with marginal revenue (MR) in Fig. 4.8.

Because the monopolist's AR curve in Fig. 4.8 is not a constant the MR is not equal to it at every point as is the case of perfect competition with its horizontal average and marginal revenue curves. In fact it will be shown below that the MR curve is twice as steep as the AR curve, where the AR curve is linear.

The quantity of output that the monopolist can sell is a function of price

$$q = f(p) \quad \text{where} \quad \frac{dq}{dp} < 0 \qquad [4.1]$$

Its inverse is given by the function

$$p = f^{-1}(q) \qquad [4.2]$$

The monopolist's total revenue is given by

$$TR = pq \qquad [4.3]$$

His MR is obtained by differentiating [4.3] with respect to q:

$$MR = \frac{dTR}{dq} = p + q \frac{dp}{dq} \qquad [4.4]$$

As $\frac{dp}{dq} < 0$ it follows that $MR < p$ (for all positive amounts of q). This means that a monopolist can only expand his output by reducing his price, in contrast to the perfect competitor who can expand his sales by as much as he likes without having to accept a reduced price.

To show that MR is twice as steep as AR simply substitute a general linear equation $p = a - bq$ into [4.3]. Thus

$$TR = qa - bq^2 \quad \text{and} \quad MR = a - 2bq.$$

Thus the MR (which a slope of $-2b$) is twice as steep as AR (with a slope of $-b$) which implies that MR declines twice as quickly as price as sales are expanded.

Another point worth noting about MR is its relation with price elasticity of demand. Price elasticity is given by

$$\epsilon = -\frac{p}{q} \cdot \frac{dq}{dp} \qquad [4.5]$$

If the numerator and the denominator are multiplied by p in [4.4] it follows that

$$MR = p \left(\frac{p}{q} + \frac{q}{p} \frac{dp}{dq} \right)$$

$$= p \left(1 - \frac{1}{\epsilon} \right) \qquad [4.6]$$

Equilibrium of the monopolist in the short run is achieved where profits are maximized:

Maximize $\pi = TR - TC$

Differentiating $\dfrac{d\pi}{dq} - \dfrac{dTR}{dq} - \dfrac{dTC}{dq} = 0$ [4.7]

$MR = MC$ [4.8]

This is shown diagramatically in Figs. 4.9 and 4.10.

Fig. 4.9

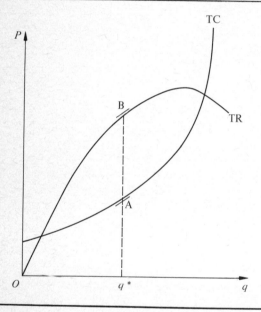

From Fig. 4.9 it is quite clear that the slopes of TR and TC are equal at q^*. This maximizes the distance between the two curves, AB. Figure 4.10 gives the other picture of equilibrium of the firm derived by sketching the marginal and average curves themselves rather than the total curves of Fig. 4.9. The profit corresponding to AB in Fig. 4.9 is given by rectangle PRST whose area is exactly equal to the distance AB.

The equilibrium described above may be long run or short run. If the AC and MC curves are shown in Fig. 4.10 are short run curves then in the long run the firm will simply change output so that it gets on to the long run average cost curve. The important point is that in such a case profits would increase. There is no entry by other firms and so all that happens in the

Fig. 4.10

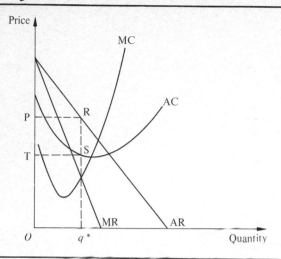

long run is that the firm merely adjusts its capacity so as to reduce its average costs and maximize profits.

Monopoly extensions

The two principal extensions to monopoly theory are price discrimination and bilateral monopoly. Price discrimination occurs when the monopolist can divide his markets on the basis of price elasticity. This difference in elasticities is what motivates price discrimination. In such cases, by selling at different prices in the different markets profits are increased. For price discrimination to be possible, however, it must be impossible for the buyers in the cheaper market to be able to resell to the more expensive market[3].

To maximize profit the price discriminating monopolist equates MC with MR in each market. Thus in a case where there are two markets denoted by AR_1, AR_2, MR_1 and MR_2 the firm's rule is $MR_1 = MR_2 = MC$[4]. To achieve this MR_1 and MR_2 are summed horizontally in Fig. 4.11 to produce ΣMR. This is then equated with MC and prices of P_1 and P_2 are read off in each market. Obviously one is higher and the other is lower than under uniform pricing. In the case of linear demand curves total output is the same whether or not discrimination is practised. With non-linear demands, however, output may be greater, less, or equal, depending on the individual AR curves[5].

The other extension of monopoly theory frequently discussed is bilateral monopoly, which exists where one producer has an output

Fig. 4.11

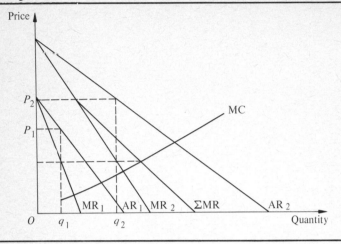

monopoly but there is only one buyer of his product. Thus bilateral monopoly corresponds to a situation where a monopolist is contracted by a "monopolist". Bilateral monopoly is illustrated in Fig. 4.12.

AR represents both the demand curve by the single buyer and the AR curve of the monopolist seller whose MR curve is shown also. MC is his marginal cost curve, such that MC = MR at A. Thus the seller monopolist

Fig. 4.12

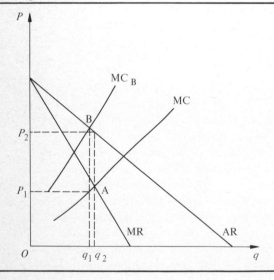

wishes to sell q_2 at a price of P_2. This is how the seller would maximize profits if he were able to induce behaviour by the single buyer equivalent to that of many buyers. The buyer, however, will not do this. He will try to control the seller. At the limit he would induce the seller to behave like a perfect competitor. Thus his MC curve would become the supply curve. If the MC curve was the supply curve the buyer would have a marginal expenses of buying the product as given by the MC_B curve. This would be equated to his demand curve (AR). Thus he would try to obtain q_1 at a price of P_1. The neoclassical approach to the indeterminacy implied is to say that prices and output would settle between P_1 and P_2 and q_1 and q_2, respectively depending on the relative bargaining skills of the two parties. Such problems have been *traditionally* regarded as beyond the scope of neoclassical economic analysis[6].

4.3 Monopolistic competition

Having examined the polar cases of market organization it now remains to look at some of the forms of market organization between these two extremes. On the surface the most obvious synthesis of the two extremes is monopolistic competition, as originated by Chamberlin (1933). This will be examined now, followed by theories of oligopoly in the next section.

Chamberlin based his theory of monopolistic competition on the empirical fact that most forms of market organization fell between the two polar cases of perfect competition and pure monopoly. He noted that there are very few monopolists because there are very few commodities which do not have close substitutes. In addition, he noted that not many commodities were homogeneous among producers. He observed the existence of "differentiated" products like whisky, cigarettes, soap, and many types of consumer durables. In some cases, the differentiation between products may consist of little more than a brand name. In cases of differentiated products, each firm has a degree of monopoly but in view of the presence of close substitutes the power to influence market prices may be very small. This differentiation of products means that industries have to be redefined. Instead of being all the firms producing a homogeneous product it is necessary in defining an industry to lump together firms in product groups, e.g., motors, tobacco, breweries, and so on.

Short run equilibrium in monopolistic competition is very similar to that of pure monopoly in the short run as illustrated in Fig. 4.10. In fact the situations are so similar that that diagram will not be repeated. The firm in monopolistic competition may make profits in the short run. The effects of the profits in this case, in contrast to monopoly, is to attract

new firms into the industry in not very different fashion from the effect of
profits in the perfectly competitive case.

It is this effect of profits in the situation of differentiated products and
Chamberlin's explanation of it that has given his theory so much significance in the literature of economics since 1933. Before examining the
nature of adjustment and equilibrium it is necessary to look at
Chamberlin's assumptions. He assumes that the firm has two demand
curves as shown in Fig. 4.13. The firm is situated initially at point E and
an output of q. It plans changing price so as to obtain greater profits. The
two demand curves DD′ and dd′ reflect the alternatives that face the firm

Fig. 4.13

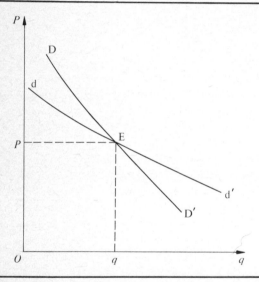

in the event that he changes his price. The firm, as a member of a large
group of firms, might feel that any reduction in price will result in a substantial increase in sales in view of the fact that any increase in output by
him will be too small in relation to the output of the industry to affect
market price. This would apply as long as all the other firms did not also
cut their prices. In the former case the demand curve facing the firm
would be dd′. However, in the latter case, where all firms reduced the
prices simultaneously the firm would have a demand curve given by DD′.
With this in mind it might prove useful if Chamberlin's assumptions
concerning demand are briefly summarized. Firstly, he assumes that there
is a large group of firms producing a differentiated product, such that *each
expects his price changes to go unnoticed by his rivals.* Secondly, for

present purposes, price alone is the variable which firms change with the intention of increasing profits. Thirdly (Chamberlin's (1933, pp. 82–3) "heroic assumption"), ". . . both demand and cost curves for all the products are uniform throughout the group". This amounts to assuming, on the cost side, that product differences are not so big as to cause cost differences.

Fig. 4.14

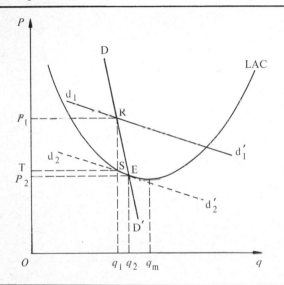

Equilibrium in the large group case with price competition is shown in Fig. 4.14 on the assumption that no new firms enter the industry. (The demand curves are as described in Fig. 4.13.) Adjustment to long run equilibrium begins at point R which is a short run equilibrium involving profits of P_1RST. Each firm on the assumption that his demand curve is given by dd' believes that he can increase his profit by reducing price. He thus reduces price, but instead of expanding his quantity demanded along dd' he moves along DD'. Alternatively shifting d_1d_1' might be regarded as sliding down DD' to d_2d_2' where long run equilibrium of E is found, and where no profits are made.

Another case which is often considered is where the number of firms within the industry may be changed in the course of moving to long run equilibrium. In Fig. 4.15 D_0D_0' is the original demand curve and LAC is the long run average cost curve. All firms in such a case reap a substantial profit the result being that firms are attracted bringing with them more

Fig. 4.15

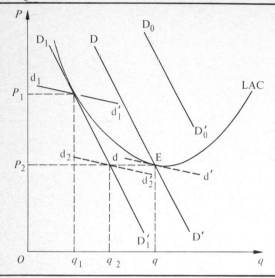

differentiated products. This has the familiar effect of causing the demand curves DD' to shift to the left; dd' also slides down until point F is reached. Equilibrium is not, however, attained at F. Because each firm thinks that d_1d_1' is its demand it will reduce price on the expectation of expanding along d_1d_1'. All firms will do the same and dd' slides down eventually to d_2d_2' where it incurs a loss. This is a temporary equilibrium. Some firms induced by the loss will leave the industry. The D_1D_1' curve will thus move to the right until equilibrium is attained at E.

4.4 Oligopoly

Oligopoly describes those market situations where there is more than one seller in a market but where there are sufficiently few sellers for the behaviour of any one seller to have an effect on the other sellers. Oligopoly then is the only case where "competition" in the popular sense of rivalry may be obviously seen to exist. In pure monopoly there is by definition no rivalry. In perfect competition there exists competition in the technical sense but not in the popular sense because the numbers of firms is so large that any one has no effect on the others. In short, there is a complete absence of rivalry. Rivalry, on the other hand, is at the very heart of oligopoly theory. The theories of oligopoly reflect (amongst other things) the well known features of rivalry — direct confrontation and conflict or "if you can't beat 'em join 'em".

The discussion will develop two main themes:

1. The "classical" solutions to oligopoly, which concentrate on the existence of stability, in situations where oligopolists "slug it out".

2. "Collusive" and "price leadership" solutions where the pugnacity of the oligopolists is often attenuated.

The famous duopoly model of Augustin Cournot

Cournot's famous model of duopoly dates from 1838 and concerns the case of two mineral water springs, which are situated side by side. One is owned by person A, the other by person B. The marginal costs of A and B

Fig. 4.16

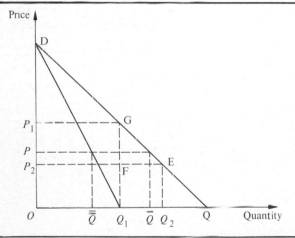

are assumed to be zero. The duopoly market is illustrated in Fig. 4.16, showing the market demand DQ and the marginal revenue curve DQ.

Initially it is assumed that A is the only seller in which case he charges the monopoly price of P_1 and sells Q_1. Next B enters the market. Cournot assumed that A never expects B to change his output and B never expects A to change his output. These behavioural assumptions are crucial. Thus when B enters the market he expects A always to sell OQ_1. He thus treats GQ as his demand curve and sells Q_1Q_2 which is the quantity which is midway between Q_1 and Q and which just equates his (linear) MR curve with MC (zero). He expects to make a profit of FEQ_2Q_1 by this policy.

On the other side A expects B always to sell $Q_1Q_2 = Q_2Q$, the slice of the market OQ_2 he regards as being available to him. He thus sells $\frac{1}{2} OQ_2$. This reduction in his output causes price to rise. B reviews the situation as a result of A's reduction in output and increases his output to $\frac{1}{2}(OQ - \frac{1}{2}OQ_2)$ which causes price to fall and induces A to review the situation.

Since A believes that B will sell $\frac{1}{2}(OQ - \frac{1}{2}OQ_2)$ the market now appears to A to be $OQ - \frac{1}{2}(OQ - \frac{1}{2}OQ_2)$. He thus reduces output again. Thus the picture has begun to emerge of A's reducing his output and B's increasing his output. The final result is that each sells $\frac{1}{3}$ of the market, i.e., $O\bar{Q}$ sold by A and $\bar{\bar{Q}}\bar{Q}$ sold by B[7].

Edgeworth's duopoly model

Another classical model of oligopoly was developed by F. Y. Edgeworth in 1897. His model was based upon the assumption that each rival assumes that the other will maintain a constant price. It assumes, as in the Cournot model, that two firms are situated alongside each other selling a homogeneous product at zero marginal cost. The total market is divided equally.

Fig. 4.17

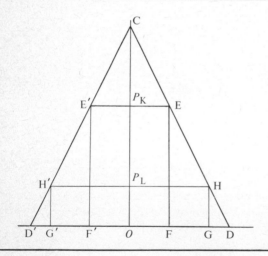

In Fig. 4.17 each firm has capacity restraints such that it cannot produce in excess of OG and OG' respectively between A and B. CD is A's demand curve and CD' is B's demand curve. A is assumed to be in the market first. He sells OF at P_K which is the position of maximum profits of $OFEP_K$. B enters the market and assumes that A will never change his price. He sets his price slightly below that of A and sells his maximum output, OG'. He thus captures a substantial proportion of A's share of the market. A's reaction to this is to lower his price, which, assuming that B will not change his price, results in his selling OG, his maximum output. This induces B to do the same and so on until the price of P_L is reached for both A and B.

However, when this price is reached there is an incentive for either firm to raise its price to P_K and reap monopoly profits. Thus A raises his price to OP_K, and B observes that if he raises his price to just below OP_K he can sell all his output and yet make greater profit. The whole process has thus started again and prices continue to move between P_L and P_K. Thus Edgeworth's duopoly solution features instability and indeterminacy.

Hotelling's model
Hotelling's model is a neoclassical model of considerable significance and much wider interest than just the types of markets for goods and services usually discussed in economic theory. Hotelling's model assumes that the duopolists have zero marginal cost in producing an identical product. The major difference in assumption is that the product is differentiated in the eyes of consumers because of the different locations of A and B. If a consumer is nearer A than B his costs of transporting the product are lower, hence his preference for a purchase from A. In particular Hotelling

Fig. 4.18

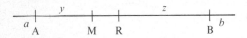

assumes that buyers are uniformly distributed along a line in Fig. 4.18. Thus a consumer located y units distance must pay the transportation costs of c per unit distance transported, making a total cost of cy per unit purchased. Hotelling also assumes that demand is completely inelastic, that the market is L units in length, and one consumer is located in each unit of length. There are a consumers to the left of A and b to the right of B as well as $y + z$ consumers between them. Thus total sales in each period are

$$L = y + z + a + b.$$

Clearly A and B have some discretion when it comes to setting their prices. For example A would never set his price so high that any of the a consumers to his left found it worth while purchasing from B and transporting goods home. A and B both have "sheltered" markets of a and b

respectively. For any particular pair of prices the $y + z$ buyers located between A and B will be divided by a point such as R in Fig. 4.18. This is because the delivered price must be equal:

$$p_A + cy - p_B + cz,$$

where p_A and p_B are A's price and B's price respectively. A's profits are $P_A(a + y)$ and B's profits are $P_B(b + z)$. If these two profit expressions are maximized stable, unique, and determinate prices always occur. This can be easily demonstrated[8].

The long run solution is more interesting. A and B can obviously relocate in the long run. A has the incentive (maximization of his sheltered market) to move as close to B as possible and B has incentive to move as close to A as possible. This results in their locating at the centre of the market M in Fig. 4.18. If A located to the right of M, B could locate just to A's left and obtain a larger sheltered market, and similarly if B located to the right of M. Thus they both locate at M.

Unlike the Cournot and Edgeworth models, the Hotelling model has some practical interest. From a welfare standpoint A and B should locate at the quartile points if transportation costs are to be minimized. Instead they locate at the median maximizing transportation costs. Thus this type of competition (rivalry) militates against ideal product differentiation. The practical implications which Hotelling draws from this are interesting. For example, he suggests that political parties are too much alike in the policies they adopt[9], and "Our cities become uneconomically large and the business districts within them are too concentrated. Methodist and Presbyterian Churches are too much alike; cider is too homogeneous." (Hotelling, 1929, p. 57.)

Price leadership and collusive solutions

The models above all assumed that the oligopoly rivals would "compete" with one another in some way. An alternative approach is that the oligopolists would recognize the fact of the interdependence and decide to "get together" in some way either by explicit arrangements such as collusion or implicit arrangements of "follow the leader". Both of these types of arrangement will be examined here.

Examples of price leadership models

Two types of model will be examined. The first of these is based upon a situation where one firm has higher costs than the other firm. The second is based upon the idea of the "dominant firm". In the first case, two firms producing a homogeneous commodity decide to split the market evenly

Fig. 4.19

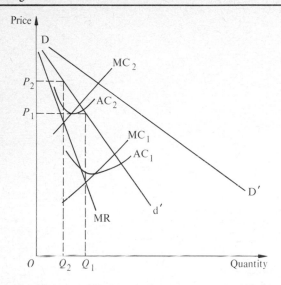

between them. In Fig. 4.19 the market demand is given by DD'. Each firm regards dd' as his demand curve and MR as his marginal revenue curve. However, their costs differ as shown by AC_1, and AC_2, etc.

Thus to maximize profits firm 1 would wish to charge P_1 and firm 2 charge P_2. In such a situation, firm 2 has no alternative but to give way and adopt firm 1's price or else he loses all his sales to firm 1. If there are substantial barriers to entry firm 1 might decide to wipe out firm 2 and therefore become a monopolist. He could probably do this by setting his price below AC_2 which would ultimately drive firm 2 out of business.

Another situation of price leadership is the so-called dominant firm case. This situation occurs where there is say one large firm in an industry and several small ones. In Fig. 4.20 the dominant firm is seen to be somewhat larger than all the other firms put together. In this case the small firms recognize the power of the dominant firm and allow it to fix the price. They thus are price-takers analogous to firms in perfect competition. The difference of course is that in the long run they do not necessarily face the zero profit solution of perfect competition.

The dominant firm has thus to solve the problem of determining price such that profits are maximized subject to the constraint that the small firms will sell all they wish at that price. In Fig. 4.20 DD' is the market demand curve and MC_F is the horizontal summation of the relevant portions of the MC curves of the small firms — the collective supply curve

Fig. 4.20

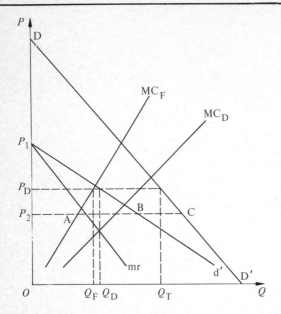

of the small firms. If the dominant firm sets his price at P_1 it sells nothing whereas if it sets it at P_2 the small firms sell P_2A and it sells AC. If this distance is plotted from P_2 to give distance $P_2B = AC$ a demand curve P_1d' can be derived for the dominant firm, with corresponding MR curve. The dominant firm thus equates MC_D and MR and sets its price at P_D. The small firms altogether produce OQ_F and total output is OQ_T.

As a preliminary to the discussion of public policy in Chapter 7 it could be noted that the contribution of such models is of considerable significance in public policy usually in the negative sense of showing the difficulties of controlling oligopolistic industries.

Collusion and cartels

Sometimes oligopolists prefer explicitly to agree on price and quantities to produce because profits can be increased by this method, rather than by competing with one another. The cartel was the popular method of doing this. A controlling body is formed by the group of firms. This then after aggregating the marginal cost curves of the individual firms fixes a price equivalent to the monopoly price. It then has to determine how much each firm should produce and, as will be noted later, has to police each firm to ensure the quantities are produced[10]. The job of policing the member firms turns out to be rather difficult because of differences in costs between member firms and because the actual determination of the quotas in each case often involve political considerations within the group. In fact it is possible for a cartel to be devised where every member has the incentive not to keep to the rules (to cheat) and so make the group worse off. This situation is best analysed by means of the prisoner's dilemma game which is a famous example of rivals acting to their mutual disadvantage.

The prisoner's dilemma

Two prisoners are separated physically. Each is told the following:

1.   If you both confess you will receive the normal punishment.

2.   If neither of you confesses you will both go free.

3.   If you confess and your fellow prisoner does not you will go free and receive an extra benefit.

4.   If you do not confess and your fellow prisoner confesses you will receive a very harsh punishment.

This is translated into a payoff matrix. The bracket figures are the payoffs — A's payoff first — (A's payoff, B's payoff).

Table 4.1

	B's strategy	
A's strategy	Confess	Don't confess
Confess	(−2, −2)	(+4, −4)
Don't confess	(−4, +4)	(+2, +2)

A looks at his position and determines his strategy. If he confesses and B confesses he loses 2. If he confesses and B does not confess he gains 4. This is obviously preferable to his other strategy which is not to confess in which event he loses 4 if B confesses and gains 2 if B does not confess. Thus when faced with two choices of gaining 4 or losing 2 and the other of gaining 2 and losing 4 it is obvious that he prefers the first of these. Hence his strategy is to confess. Similar reasoning applies to B who will therefore also confess. Thus both prisoners have ended up by confessing even though it would be mutually desirable for neither to do so!

The same sort of problem can apply to cartels. Just as with the prisoners it was mutually desirable for neither of them to confess, in the case of firms their mutual interest might be to abide by terms of the agreement of the cartel. However, the temptation to break the agreement may be so great that all members of the group end up by cheating. In Fig. 4.21 DD′ is

Fig. 4.21

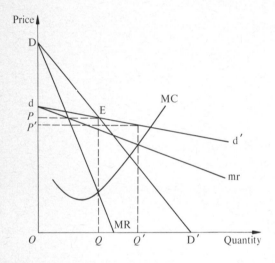

the firm's demand curve, under the assumption that all firms will charge the same price. Thus their prices move together. The corresponding marginal revenue curve is shown as MR. Point E is therefore the equilibrium for the firm that would be established by the collusive group. Price cutting (cheating) might appear attractive to the firm if it believed that the other firms in the group would not cheat. The demand curve in this case is given by dd′, with its marginal revenue curve mr. If the firm believed this to be his demand curve it would be induced to cheat and reduce its price to P'. In view of the high demand elasticity the temptation to cheat is considerable in this case.

A payoff matrix similar to Table 4.1 in the prisoners' dilemma game is shown in Table 4.2. The matrix shows that it is mutually beneficial for firms to collude. However, as is the case of the earlier prisoners' dilemma, each ends up by cheating and therefore losing out. Thus in collusive

Table 4.2

	B's strategy	
A's strategy	Collude	Cheat
Collude	(160, 160)	(0, 200)
Cheat	(200, 0)	(100, 100)

oligopoly stability is clearly not guaranteed. Thus cartels have gone in for all sorts of devices to police and punish members who cheat in an attempt to preserve the cartel.

The likelihood that collusion will be unstable is increased if the firms involved have differing costs. In such cases it is possible for firms to agree on a price and output combinations that maximizes joint profits but not possible for them to agree a share-out amongst the group of this output. Maximizing joint profits would imply that the high-cost firms produced less than the low-cost firms. This might prove unsatisfactory to the high-cost firms who desire a larger share of the market. Thus devices like royalties payable by the low-cost firms into a central pool to compensate the high-cost firms might be devised. However, these arrangements could prove unsatisfactory to the low-cost firms who might become tired of subsidizing their higher-cost brethren.

Limit pricing
The analysis of the previous section assumed that the firms only had to agree amongst themselves and then stick to their bargain. There was no question of a threat from outside the group through entry of new firms. The possibility of entry by new firms is quite a usual threat with which oligopolists have the benefit of barriers to entry which mean that newcomers can enter only by getting over these barriers. This is depicted analytically in the framework of the theory of the firm by the new firms having higher costs than the existing firms. Thus in terms of Fig. 4.22 the costs of new firms are shown as being higher than those of the existing firms. (For simplicity horizontal average cost curves are employed.) The AR curve is the long run industry demand curve, which is assumed to be unchanging over time.

The effect of the barriers to entry, as shown in Fig. 4.22, is to keep new firms out as long as the price set by the existing firms does not exceed OA. Effectively then the demand curve facing existing firms is ABG (with

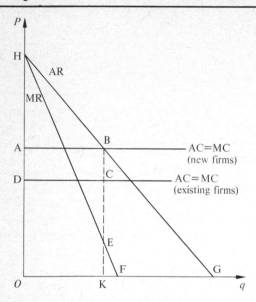

corresponding discontinuous marginal revenue curve ABEF). Thus with this effective demand curve existing firms would equate marginal revenue and marginal cost at C which would imply a price of OA and profit of ABCD. This would enable profits to be made and at the same time prevent entry.

Such a simple static model is quite interesting in that it provides a simple illustration of the benefits of barriers to entry which fall short of the barriers to entry of pure monopoly. However, the analysis does nothing to answer the problems posed in the previous section regarding the instability of collusion. To these problems shoud be added the problems which arise when dynamic considerations are taken into account. The existing firms face the problem with barriers to entry that another alternative to preventing entry is available. They, in fact, may set price above OA and, in the short run, make profits in excess of ABCD. However, the entry of new firms means that long run profits per firm are reduced, and excess capacity results which increases the likelihood of damaging price cutting by the firm along the lines of the previous section[11]. Even so, a case where the time-scale for building capacity is relatively long and the barriers to entry do not offer a very significant cost advantage to existing firms, could occur in which the discounted stream of higher profits now and lower profits later exceeded the benefits to be gained from the level of profits which resulted from restricting entry[12].

Exercises — 4

1.   What would happen if all firms were initially producing q_1 on SAC_1 in Fig. 4.4?

2.   Show, that the Hessian of the production function is singular when the production function is linear homogeneous. Show the implications of the case where all factor prices are constant for the attainment of a maximum by the firm.

3.   The demand function facing a certain profit maximizing monopolist is

$$x = 100 - 2p,$$

where x is the amount of the commodity which he can sell per unit of time at a price of p. His total costs per period of time, C, are given by the relation

$$C = 500 + 10x.$$

Find the values of the following in the optimum position:

(a)   Marginal revenue, MR;
(b)   output, x;
(c)   price charged, p;
(d)   total revenue, TR;
(e)   total variable cost, VC;
(f)   total cost, C;
(g)   total profit, Π.
(h)   elasticity of demand, η.

4.   Now suppose the government imposes a lump sum tax of (i) 400 and (ii) 900 per period of time on the monopolist.
(a)   What will the firm's *output, price*, and *profit* be in the short run?
(b)   What will he do in the long run, assuming that before the tax he was in long run equilibrium?

5.   Assume that a monopolist's total demand comes from what are really two quite separate markets, between which it would be prohibitively costly to transfer this commodity. These two markets have demand functions,

$$x_1 = 40 - \tfrac{2}{3}p_1 \qquad x_2 = 60 - \tfrac{4}{3}p_2$$

respectively and total cost is given by $TC = 500 + \tfrac{1}{8}x^2$.

(A)   In order to maximize total profits;

(a)   what price will he charge in each market;

(b)   what quantity of the commodity will he sell to each market;

(c)   what will be the elasticity of demand in each market in the equilibrium position;

(d)   what will be his total profit?

(B)   Compare the above values of total output, total profit, the two prices, and the two elasticities with the corresponding values when he does *not* discriminate. Do you think the change in each case is or is not typical? Give your reasons in each case.

6.   In perfect competition the supply curve for an individual firm is derived by equating price and marginal cost where MC is above average variable cost. Derive the supply relationship for a monopolist where

$$TC = 500 + \frac{x^2}{8}$$

$$AR = 50 - \frac{x}{2}$$

Is it possible to derive a supply curve for monopoly?

7.   Show from the Hotelling model that maximizing A's profit and B's profit yields prices of

$$P_A = c \left(L + \frac{a - b}{3} \right)$$

$$P_B = c \left(L - \frac{a - b}{3} \right)$$

Hint: First use the expression in the text for total sales and the condition that delivered prices are equal to derive the expressions for each firm's profit. Recalling that each entrepreneur assumes that his rival will not change his price these expressions are maximized.

8.   Show that the Cournot solution converges at each firm taking one third of the market.

Notes

1.   In this case optimal plant size simply means optimal in the sense that q_2 is produced at minimum average cost.

2.   This is discussed further in Crew and Rowley (1970). An example would be a public utility like gas, electricity, water, or telephones.

3.   This is a simplifying assumption used in the theory. Practical applications require that it is costly for buyers to transfer between markets and that it is not prohibitively expensive for the firm to maintain its barriers between the markets or market segments as they are sometimes called. A practical illustration of discrimination illustrating these points are the rates of individual and library subscription charged by many publishers for professional and academic journals.

4.   This can easily be demonstrated by simple calculus

$$\text{Max } \pi = TR_1(q_1) + TR_2(q_2) - TC(q_1 - q_2)$$

differentiating partially with respect to q_1 and q_2

$$\frac{\partial \pi}{\partial q_1} = MR_1 - \frac{\partial TC(q_1 + q_2)}{\partial q_1} = 0$$

$$\frac{\partial \pi}{\partial q_2} = MR_2 - \frac{\partial TC(q_1 + q_2)}{\partial q_2} = 0$$

which yields $MR_1 = MC$, $MR_2 = MC$.

This follows because $\dfrac{\partial TC}{\partial q_1} = \dfrac{\partial TC}{\partial q_2}$

This can be shown as follows

$$TC = F(q_1, q_2)$$

Write $TC = F(q)$,   where $q = q_1 + q_2$.

Differentiate with respect to q_1 and q_2 (using function of a function rule)

$$\frac{dTC}{dq} \cdot \frac{\partial q}{\partial q_1} \quad \text{and} \quad \frac{\partial TC}{\partial q} \cdot \frac{\partial q}{\partial q_2}$$

These are equal because

$$\frac{\partial q}{\partial q_1} = \frac{\partial q}{\partial q_2}.$$

5.   The proof of this result is rather involved and of mainly historical interest. For a full proof see Robinson (1933, pp. 188–95), or Edwards (1950).

6.   For example Ferguson (1969, p. 282) well summarizes the approach: "The precise result is determined by factors beyond the purview of economic analysis." However, more recently a difference of approach can be noted with economic analysis attempting to wrestle with the problems of bargaining, e.g., Cross (1969) and Coddington (1968).

7.   Consider B who sells $Q_1Q_2 = Q_2Q = \frac{1}{2}OQ_1$ which is a quarter of the market. He next increases his output to

$$\frac{1}{2}(OQ - \frac{1}{2}OQ_2) = \frac{1}{2}(OQ - \frac{3}{8}OQ) = (\frac{1}{2} - \frac{3}{16}) OQ = \frac{5}{16}OQ.$$

He has then expanded by $\frac{1}{16}OQ$. His next expansion would be by $\frac{1}{64}$. (As an exercise (Exercise 8) the reader is encouraged to work out a few more terms of the series and show that B's final output is $\frac{1}{3}OQ$.)

8.   The reader is encouraged to do just this in Exercise 7 at the end of the chapter.

9.   The work of Downs (1956) develops this approach when he argues that political parties try to occupy the centre ground. Hotelling's paper is then an important forerunner of Downs and other important work which goes under the title of the *economics of politics*.

10.   There is also the loose cartel which is much more common. This involves setting a price and allowing members to sell all they want at these prices. Examples of this include scale fees by lawyers, physicians, and other professional men. Such agreement may be simply tacit, e.g., oil companies and petrol prices.

11.   On the assumption that output OK is equal to capacity of the existing firms the entry of new firms is bound to create excess capacity.

12.   For a discussion of the behaviour of collusive firms in such situations and the answer to questions like when the industry price should be set equal to the limit price see Wenders (1971).

5

Motivation and decision making

The neoclassical theory of the firm, with its assumption that the firm's objective is to maximize profit, and the resulting theories of market situations bear little resemblance to the organizations which are known as firms in modern economies. Several alternatives to the neoclassical model have been proposed. Principally these argue that firms are complex organizations which have to be "managed". This problem, the management problem, is solved by the recruitment of a special type of employee called management, the effect of which is drastically to attenuate the profit maximization motivation. Owing to the special importance of management in such cases the theories relevant to such firms are, not surprisingly, called *managerial theories of the firm*. However, before examining such theories it is useful briefly to indicate some of the methodological defences for the use of the neoclassical theory. The principal argument would be that abstraction requires simplification of complex reality if analysis and prediction are to be possible. This is particularly relevant in the case of competitive situations. In such situations the pressures are such that firms have no viable alternative other than adopting profit maximization as an objective, and in such cases the neoclassical theory provides adequate predictions on prices, etc. Indeed, alternative more complex theories would be judged as redundant on the grounds that simpler theories are available[1]. Thus the theories which will be set out in this chapter would appear to be relevant mainly to situations where competition is imperfect, and especially to situations of oligopoly and monopoly.

There is a considerable body of literature on managerial theories of the firm. This chapter will examine certain contributions which summarize the work in major areas. The contributions of Williamson (1967), Baumol (1967), and Marris (1964) on managerial discretion will be examined in section 5.1. In section 5.2 the behavioural contributions of Cyert and March (1963), Simon (1957, 1959, 1964), Baumol and Quandt (1964), Baumol and Stewart (1971), and Day (1967) will be examined. In section 5 3 two quasi-neoclassical theories developed in the one case by Crew, Jones-Lee, and Rowley (1971), and in the other case by Williamson (1970) will be examined. Finally section 5.4 is concerned with a brief critique of the theories.

5.1 Managerial theories

The managerial discretion theory of the firm developed by Williamson (1967), the sales-maximizing theory developed by Baumol, and the growth-maximizing theory developed by Marris all place managers and managerial motivation in a central place. Modern firms are highly complex systems with considerable problems of control and organization. Thus the function of managing these complex systems cannot be borne by one man and the functions of the neoclassical entrepreneur have to be shouldered by two largely disjoint groups, managers and shareholders. The latter desire a maximum return on their investment and therefore, like the entrepreneur of neoclassical economics, want profits to be maximized. The managers, of course, are also concerned with profits; in so far as management is a profession, and they are charged with the stewardship of shareholder's money, they are concerned with maximizing profits. On the other hand, to the extent that they are men with power and discretion in an organization and to the extent that they perhaps only gain to a minor degree by increases in profit, as this goes to increase the shareholder's equity, they may have other considerations other than profits in their utility functions as managers. For example, they would certainly be interested in their own emoluments, and they are likely to find certain kinds of expenditure more attractive than other kinds. Williamson cites as an example of the latter expenditure on staff. Obviously a manager seems likely to prefer a pretty secretary and a carpeted private office to alternative arrangements which involve a typing pool or a less well-appointed office. To the extent that pressure from the capital market and competition in the product market is imperfect the manager therefore has discretion to pursue goals other than profits. The Williamson, Baumol, and Marris theories are concerned with the motivation of management and the implications of managerial motivation in the theory of the firm.

Williamson's managerial discretion theory
The basic rationale of Williamson's theory is perhaps more graphically summarized in his own words:

"*. . . in the absence of rigorous competition in the product market and* *where the separation of ownership from control is substantial, there is no compelling reason to assume that the firm is operated so as to maximize profit. On the contrary, such behaviour would appear to require an unusual variety of rationality — and one not widely found in human affairs — namely, a complete detachment of individual interests from occupational decision-making. Thus . . . where discretion in the decision-making unit exists, this will ordinarily be exercised in a fashion that reflects the individual interests of the decision-makers."* (Williamson, 1967, p. 55.)

Williamson had three components to his models of "expense" preference,

(i) expenditure on staff,
(ii) expenditure on emoluments, and
(iii) discretionary profit.

There is a tendency to value staff for reasons other than their contribution to productivity. For example modern organizations generate insecurity amongst members[2]. Sometimes the best way to guarantee survival seems to be sheer size. Hence this situation would promote the manager's desire to expand his staff. A manager might also feel that it is desirable to give his staff opportunities for personal development. Thus efforts will be made to expand the uses of staff, again pointing towards expanding staff. A manager's interest in emoluments is obvious. Since management has discretion in this matter it would not be surprising if there existed a rent portion of management emoluments which if removed would not result in a manager seeking alternative employment. Exactly how such emoluments were taken, in the form of extra salary or perquisites, would depend to some extent on tax considerations. However, it is the total not the breakdown of the emoluments between salary and perquisites which is relevant. Hence Williamson's model concentrates on the total of emoluments. Discretionary profit is considered important for management. If management produced zero economic profit the firm would be making the minimum profit consistent with survival. This might result in pressures on management which they would prefer to do without. However, management would also prefer to avoid making maximum profit as this would mean that no discretionary expenditure had taken place. Thus management chooses a position between these bounds[3]. Depending on the extent to which shareholders can monitor and control management's performance, they may be able to insure that management operates the firm at a level above the lower band of survival mentioned above. Thus a profit constraint is imposed on managers in Williamson's theory and any profits made by the management in excess of this he terms "discretionary profits".

The staff and emoluments model

Williamson's original work on the subject involved construction and detailed discussion of three models,

(i)   a staff model,
(ii) an emoluments model, and
(iii) a staff and emoluments model.

His model (iii) incorporated the development of models (i) and (ii) to provide a model which he is concerned with extending and testing in the rest of his book. In view of the more general nature of model (iii) only this model will be examined in detail here.

The terms in Williamson's model are defined as follows:

$$R = \text{revenue} = PX; \; \partial^2 R/\partial X \partial S \geqslant 0$$

$$P = \text{price} = P(X, S, E); \; \partial P/\partial X \leqslant 0; \; \partial P/\partial S \geqslant 0; \; \partial P/\partial E \geqslant 0$$

$$X = \text{output}$$

$$S = \text{expenditure on staff}$$

$$E = \text{the state of the environment (in particular a demand shift}$$
$$\text{parameter)}$$

$$C = \text{production cost} = C(X)$$

$$M = \text{managerial emoluments}$$

$$\Pi = R - C - S = \text{actual profit}$$

$$\Pi_R = \Pi - M = \text{reported profit}$$

$$T = \text{taxes, where } t = \text{tax rate}, \; \bar{T} = \text{lump sum tax}$$

$$\Pi_O = \text{minimum (after tax) profit required}$$

$$\Pi_R - \Pi_O - T = \text{discretionary profit}$$

$$U = \text{the utility function.}$$

The positive preference of the management of the firm for staff, emoluments and profit is incorporated in the utility function as follows:

Maximize: $U = U(S, M, \Pi_R - \Pi_O - T)$ [5.1]

Subject to: $\Pi_R \geqslant \Pi_O + T$ [5.2]

Williamson, by adopting the familiar assumption of diminishing marginal utility, and disallowing corner solutions, concludes that the firm will always choose values of the decision variables S, M and $\Pi_R - \Pi_O - T$ which yield positive utility with respect to each component. Thus $\Pi_R - \Pi_O - T$ will always be positive. The constraint [5.2] can be re-written as $\Pi_R - \Pi_O - T \geqslant 0$. Williamson's argument thus implies that it will always be satisfied by an inequality and is therefore redundant. This enables him to handle the problem as a straightforward unconstrained maximization problem. The functional relationships for profit are substituted into [5.1] to yield

Maximize $U = U(S, M, (1 - t)(R - C - S - M - \bar{T}) - \Pi_O)$ [5.3]

The first order conditions are[4]

$$\frac{\partial R}{\partial X} = \frac{\partial C}{\partial X}$$ [5.4]

$$\frac{\partial R}{\partial S} = \frac{-U_1 + (1 - t)U_3}{(1 - t)U_3}$$ [5.5]

$$U_2 = (1 - t)U_3$$ [5.6]

Equation [5.4] shows that production decisions are made along profit maximizing lines, by equating marginal cost and marginal revenue[5].

Equation [5.5] can be rearranged to yield $\frac{\partial R}{\partial S} = 1 - \frac{1}{1 - t}\frac{U_1}{U_3}$ which indicates that staff in excess of the profit maximizing quantity are employed. (Profit maximization would obviously demand that extra expenditure on staff was incurred up to the point where $\frac{\partial R}{\partial S} = 1$ on its marginal value product was equal to its marginal cost.) Equation [5.6] shows that the firm absorbs some actual profit as emolument, the actual amount depending upon the tax rate.

Williamson also derived comparative statics properties of this model and these are given in Table 5.1, where a plus sign means that the parameter and variable concerned move up or down together, and a negative sign

Table 5.1   Comparative statics properties of Williamson's Staff-emoluments model

		Parameter		
		E	t	$\bar{T}$
Variable	X^O	+	+ ?	−
	S^O	+	+ ?	−
	M^O	+	+ ?	−

means that they move in opposite directions[6]. The results are clearly interesting, and different from that of the profit maximizing firm whose comparative statics properties are given in Table 5.2. (Notice that, because the profit maximizing firm does not absorb any profits as emoluments, M^0 has been omitted from Table 5.2.)

Table 5.2   Comparative statics properties of the profit maximization model

		Parameter		
		E	t	$\bar{T}$
Variable	X^0	+	0	0
	S^0	+	0	0

The different effects of the taxes on staff expenditures and emoluments is particularly interesting. Increasing lump-sum taxes ($\bar{T}$) results in a reduction in output (X), a lower expenditure on staff (S) and a lower level of emoluments (M). In contrast the effect of an increase in corporation taxes (t) is (ambiguously) to cause the decision variables to be increased. Williamson conducted a detailed graphical analysis to explain this ambiguity. The situation can best be visualized by considering firstly the case where the firm is not hard pressed to satisfy its minimum profit constraint. In this case, the substitution effect of t makes profits more expensive in terms of emoluments and staff. Hence the firm is likely to spend more on staff and emoluments. However, if the effect of the corporation tax is so severe that the firm finds it difficult to meet its profit constraint, the income effect is such that it might reduce staff and emoluments in order to meet the profit constraint.

Thus the Williamson theory of managerial discretion shows that values for price, output, staff expenditures, and emoluments are likely to be very different from those predicted by the profit maximizing model. The comparative statics properties of the models are also different, the effects of taxes being of particular interest. Some of the implications of these results for public policy terms will be discussed in Chapter 7.

Baumol's sales revenue maximizing model
Baumol's sales revenue maximization model is a managerial theory of the firm in the sense that it owes its origin, like the Williamson theory, to its

author's view of managerial motivation. Baumol's views originated from his own not inconsiderable dealings with managers and businessmen as a consultant. He was impressed by the importance they placed upon sales staff. "In my dealings with them I have been struck with the importance the oligopolistic enterprises attach to the value of their sales." (Baumol, 1967, p. 45.) Thus like Williamson's theory, the Baumol's theory is managerial and oligopolistic.

Baumol, like Williamson, gave a number of justifications for his theory. He argued that businessmen attach great importance to the magnitude of sales and view with considerable concern the prospect of declining sales. This concern often stems from the attitude of consumers who might shun a product whose sales appear to be declining, thus accelerating the decline. Similarly banks, creditors, and the capital market are likely to be less keen on firms with declining sales. The firm's own distributors might also get restive in the event of declining sales. Declining sales are likely to necessitate reductions in personnel, which might have the effect of making relations more difficult within the firm. Additionally, the scale of the operation often influences the amount of executive salaries in firms. *Ceteris paribus*, higher sales are likely to result in high executive salaries.

Like Williamson, Baumol also argues that firms do not go for sales at the expense of everything else. They are also concerned with profit. Thus they will not produce at an output which maximizes revenue if this output involves the firm operating at a loss. Baumol argued therefore that the firm needs a minimum profit, and that as long as this constraint is met the firm will aim to maximize sales. This minimum profit level is determined not only on the basis of the firm's need to maximize sales in the current period but also upon its needs to sustain growth of sales. Profits are required for this purpose, either in the form of retained earnings or new capital from the market. Obviously the larger the profits made by the firm the easier it will be to raise finance in the market, and the easier it will be to find resources from internal sources. Thus the firm has a familiar tradeoff problem. It wants profits, particularly to finance future sales, but increased current sales (as will be noted below) can only be achieved by reductions in profit. Thus the firm is likely to choose some level of profit between maximum profit and the profit level corresponding to maximum sales. Finally, there is the shareholder/capital market influence which the firm must face. The firm will not wish a substantial fall in the share price. Thus, aside from the managers' own objectives, there will be pressure from the market to insure that the firms earn a certain level of profit.

Baumol's approach to his sales maximizing model is to argue that the firm maximizes sales subject to a profit constraint. The approach, which is illustrated graphically below, consists of incorporating a minimum profit constraint in the objective function by setting up a Lagrangian as follows:

Maximize sales $= R = P \cdot Q$

Subject to $\quad \Pi \geqslant \Pi^o$

Setting up a Lagrangian this gives

Maximize $L = R + \lambda(R - C - \Pi^o)$

where $\quad C = C(Q) =$ total cost

$\quad\quad\quad \Pi^o =$ required profit level

First order conditions are

$$\frac{dR}{dQ} = -\lambda \left(\frac{dR}{dQ} - \frac{dC}{dQ} \right)$$

or $\dfrac{1 + \lambda}{\lambda} \dfrac{dR}{dQ} = \dfrac{dC}{dQ}$ [5.7]

Thus from [5.7] where $\lambda > 0$ MR $<$ MC. Baumol argues that the constraint will always be binding and $\lambda > 0$ implying MR $<$ MC[7].

Fig. 5.1

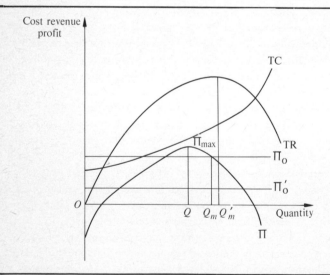

A simple graphical analysis of the above result is now given. Figure 5.1 shows total cost, total revenue, total profit (Π), together with the profit constraint (Π_o). The firm achieves optimality at Q_m where total profit is just equal to the constraint. It is clear from examination of the slopes of the total cost and total revenue curves that at this point MR < MC. Notice that if the profit constraint were only Π_0' that the firm would produce Q_m'. However, as argued above, when other decisions, e.g., advertising, are taken into account the profit constraint will always be binding so this situation where sales are at a maximum at R_m is of restricted interest. Output is of course in excess of the profit maximizing output which is given by OQ. Only in the event of the profit constraint becoming very severe and equal to Π max, the profit maximizing profit, would the sales maximizing firm produce the same output as the profit maximizing firm.

Fig. 5.2

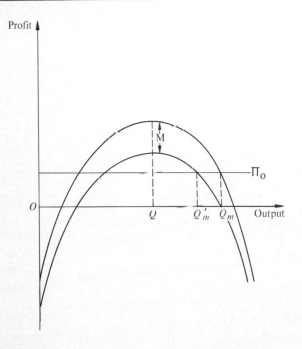

The effect of a lump sum tax can be shown quite simply from the total profit curve (Π). In Fig. 5.2 the profit before the imposition of a tax is given by Π, and the profit constraint is shown as Π_0. The effect of a lump-sum tax on the firm of amount M is to make the firm cut back its output to OQ_m'. This follows because the new profit curve Π' cuts the constraint, Π_0, corresponding to output OQ_m'. Thus, like the Williamson model, the lump-sum tax in Baumol's model causes output to be affected, in contrast to the predictions of the neoclassical theory which would predict an unchanged output at OQ.

Baumol also analyses input combinations. In this case, however, efficient input combinations are employed in just the same way as they are in the case of the profit maximizing firm. Thus where total revenue for a profit maximizing firm and for a sales maximizing firm happen to be equal each firm will use identical quantities of the same inputs and employ them

Fig. 5.3

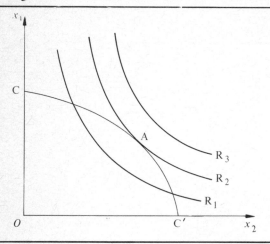

in exactly the same way. A simple diagrammatic argument can be used to illustrate this point. In Fig. 5.3, x_1 and x_2 represent quantities of inputs X_1, and X_2[8].

R_1, R_2, etc., are isorevenue curves for x_1, and x_2. Thus R_1 is the locus of points x_1 and x_2 which provide revenue of R_1. Similarly CC' represents all combinations of x_1 and x_2 corresponding to a fixed outlay (total cost). In such a case profit maximization would be at point tangency A. However, point A is also the highest attainable isorevenue curve and therefore the maximum revenue or sales-maximizing point.

Marris on "managerial capitalism"

Marris (1964) is a theory of the growth of the firm based upon some assumptions regarding managerial discretion, which are somewhat similar to the notions of managerial discretion developed by Williamson. The first chapters of Marris's book relate to the institutional framework and to answering the question of why (managerial) firms are different from entrepreneurial or neoclassical firms. He argues that the modern corporation has many of the features of "bureaucratic" organizations like the Civil Service. Thus some of the central control of salaries that is present in the Civil Service is present in firms. In this kind of organization it would appear quite reasonable to argue that executives do everything they can to promote the growth and security of the firm. For instance, Marris argues the executive's salary and status depends to a large extent on the size of his department. The executive tends to be judged by his peers, his subordinates, and particularly his superiors for his professional competence. Since his contribution to profit would often be very difficult to assess some other method of evaluating him has to be arrived at. Thus how he rubs along with other people, how smoothly he runs his department become important means of evaluating his performance. He also needs to show something more than this to raise himself in his colleagues' eyes. This something extra is normally his success in expanding the activities of the firm and in particular the activities under him. In so doing he also aims at — and stands a good chance of — making his position and that of his subordinates more secure. Thus seen as a quasi-bureaucratic organization the firm rewards those who contribute toward its growth and security[9].

Out of his institutional framework Marris (1964, 1971) develops a number of models and raises some interesting issues which are discussed further in Chapter 7. In particular, he analyses the means by which the firm can use its market power to achieve its growth objectives. One of these, which is also discussed by Lombardini (1971), is the power of the firm to grow by expanding into new markets some of which come from the "creation" of new products and new demands in the minds of consumers. In common with Baumol and Williamson, he argues that the capital market places restraints on the pursuit of these goals. He particularly emphasizes the threat of takeover.

The firm has to live with the threat of a raid based upon Marris's assumption of the ever-presence of a potential raider. Thus Marris argues that the firm must needs incorporate its valuation ratio — the ratio of the market value of the equity capital to the book value of the equity assets — into its utility function[10].

5.2 Behavioural theories of the firm

The principal exponents of the behavioural theory of the firm were Simon (1954, 1964) and Cyert and March (1963) whose work at Carnegie Institute of Technology from the middle 1950s onwards was important for the new approaches to the theory of the firm which it is stimulated. One highly significant effect of the behavioural school was to reopen a meaningful interest by economists into the internal organization of firms[11]. Along with this interest came the suggestion by Leibenstein that internal inefficiency of the firm was likely to be much more significant than the familiar allocative inefficiency which arises in monopoly when price exceeds marginal cost, as discussed in Chapter 4.

Leibenstein (1966) coined the phrase X-efficiency to describe this internal inefficiency[12] . The previous neoclassical analysis virtually ignored X-inefficiency or assumed it away. The very nature of profit maximization in the neoclassical firm was such that X-inefficiency was disallowed[13]. The firm could not at the same time make maximum profits and be X-inefficient. The behavioural theories by directing attention to internal aspects of the firm therefore provide important insights into the possibilities of X-inefficiency within the firm. The summary of behavioural theories which follows will emphasize this point.

Cyert and March's behavioural theorizing
Cyert and March's behavioural theory of the firm represents in part an attempt to deal with the problem of uncertainty and the firm. Alchian (1950) summarized the situation very well:

"Attacks on this (neoclassical profit maximization) are widespread, but only one attack has been really damaging, that of G. Tintner. He denies that profit maximization ever makes any sense where there is uncertainty. Uncertainty arises from at least two sources: imperfect foresight and human inability to solve complex problems containing a host of variables even when an optimum is definable. Tintner's proof is simple. Under uncertainty by definition, each action that may be chosen is identified with a distribution of potential outcomes, not with a unique outcome. Implicit in uncertainty is the consequence that these distributions of potential outcomes are overlapping. It is worth emphasis that each possible action has a distribution of potential outcomes, only one of which will materialize if the action is taken, and that one outcome cannot be foreseen. Essentially, the task is converted into making a decision (selecting an action) whose potential outcome distribution is preferable, that is, choosing the action with the optimum distribution since there is no such thing as a maximizing distribution."[14]

Cyert and March (1963) tackled the above problem of the lack of uniqueness of profit maximization by studying the way businessmen make decisions under conditions of uncertainty. Indeed they argue that ". . . in order to understand contemporary economic decision making we need to supplement the study of market factors with an examination of the internal operation of the firm." (p. 1.) This involves understanding the process by which decision rules are learned and the ways in which such rules are changed in the light of feedback from the environment.

Some of the main elements of their work will now be summarized. This will be followed by an examination of some extensions and applications of their analysis and a discussion of its significance.

Cyert and March draw heavily on organization theory in constructing their behavioural theory of the firm. This aims to be a theory of the firm in the sense of the neoclassical theory in that it focuses on economic decisions (price and output). This turned out to be no trivial task because organization theory did not focus on problems that were specifically economic.

Cyert and March argue that it is fruitful to analyse the process of decision making in the firm in terms of variables that affect organizational goals, organizational expectations, and organizational choice. It might seem difficult to envisage how organizations can have goals. Clearly individuals have goals but it is not obvious that an organization has goals. However, when an organization is viewed as a coalition (or managers, workers, shareholders, suppliers, and so on) then it becomes easier to envisage its having goals, especially when goals are regarded as the product of a bargaining-learning process between the members of the coalition. A coalition exists because side payments are available for distribution between members. The actual amount of total side payments is not fixed and depends on the form taken by the coalition. Some side payments may be in cash or kind but more often than not side payments take the form of policy side payments, which are the right to some say in policy of the organization. The bargaining process of goal formation is constantly subject to review. This is because individuals' aspiration levels change with experience. The process of "satisficing" provides a good illustration of how aspiration levels are modified. "Satisfactory" levels of performance are set. If these are exceeded then the aspirations are raised and so are the satisfactory levels of performance. Similarly, if they were not achieved they are lowered subsequently. Conflicting objectives are reconciled by a similar adjustment process. For example, one department may wish the product better tailored to individual needs, while another department wishes for greater standardization. Such conflicts are sometimes resolved by sequentially tackling the goals concerned. In addition, bargaining might occur so that two inconsistent goals are reconciled by adopting satisfactory standards of performance in each case. Furthermore, inside the organization the information is often not generated which makes the mutual inconsistency of certain goals stand out.

Thus very considerable differences between this theory and the theory of the firm have already appeared. A very important aspect is that maximizing has been replaced by satisficing. Another feature is that in most organizations the side payments made are usually in excess of those necessary to keep the coalition together. Where this excess occurs Cyert and March would say that *organization slack* is present. Some of this might represent a rent payment but other parts of it might simply be internal inefficiency (X-inefficiency).

Some features of the way in which organizations adapt themselves to change and organize themselves for the solution of problems are stressed by Cyert and March. These are summarized below as motivation for the models of economic decision making which they produce. One very important feature of the firm's decision process is its use of standard operating procedures. Such procedures are employed to avoid uncertainty. They therefore feature feedback which brings in particular decision rules. These rules themselves are maintained and observed. A feature of organizations is their caution regarding change. The rules involve recording and reporting as well as specifying what is acceptable performance. There are also rules regarding information which is to be produced and where it is to go; they also involve planning. A major planning device in the firm is budgeting which features many rules.

Thus the Cyert and March firm might be seen as an organization having multiple, changing, acceptable goals. When these goals are satisfied, the firm jogs along with organization slack. However, if they are not satisfied a trigger mechanism is set off which promotes search for alternatives, which is intensified if failure persists. The firm seeks to avoid uncertainty by adopting regular procedures and responding to feedback. Similarly, it makes choices and decisions by various rules of thumb and standard operating procedures.

An illustration of the implications of this for economic decisions is now given by examination of their models. They applied their theorizing to three models of pricing in a department store, a mark-up model for ordinary pricing, a "sales" model for the regular "sales" held by the firm, and a mark-down model where drastic action was required. The first two of these deal with ordinary behaviour and routine decisions of the firm and the third deals with the "crisis" type situation, albeit of a relatively minor or not unanticipated kind, which triggers off the search mentioned above. The mark-up model and mark-down model will therefore be discussed below because they illustrate both main aspects of their theory and also because these models have been subject to further testing and scrutinizing[15]. Cyert and March's mark-up model is simply "divide each cost by 0.6 . . . and move to the nearest $0.95" (p. 38). On exclusive lines (lines unavailable to the competition) the rate was modified by moving to the next $0.95. Of 197 predicted prices, 188 were correct to the cent using this rule. Baumol and Stewart found that the Cyert and March rule did not predict successfully when they tested it against data seven years later.

They found, however, that a 45-per cent mark-up operated in 60 per cent of cases. The mark-down model operated in "crisis" situations where it was necessary say to get rid of overstocked merchandise or remnants, and the stock situation was such that they could not wait for the regular sale period. A complete model in the form of a flow chart is shown in Cyert and March (1963, pp. 144–5). However, the basic rule can be summarized as follows,

"The general rule for first mark-downs is to reduce the retail price by $\frac{1}{3}$ and carry the result down to the nearest . . . $0.85. There are some exceptions. Where the ending constraint forces too great a deviation from the $\frac{1}{3}$ rule (e.g., where the regular price is $5.00 or less), ad hoc procedures are occasionally adopted. On higher-priced items a 40 per cent mark-down is taken. On a few items manufacturers maintain price control. Occasionally, items represent a closeout of a manufacturer's line and a greater mark-down is taken." (p. 143.)

Cyert and March's test (involving 159 prices) of the mark-down model predicted correctly in 88 per cent of cases using their own tests. It was, in view of the relative crisis nature of such decisions, not quite as good as their other two models at 95-per cent and 96-per cent accuracy. Baumol and Stewart's test of the Cyert and March rules together with a few modifications of their own revealed 73-per cent correct predictions. The Baumol and Stewart tests, therefore, tend to confirm that much routine economic decision making is on the basis of rules of thumb.

One interesting aspect of this is that the mark-up seemed to have a tendency to increase over time. At first sight this might seem hard to justify. Inflation, for example, would be taken care of in the increase in the cost of the product. The margin would just be added onto this higher cost and this gives no explanation why the margin should rise. The explanation, Baumol and Stewart argue, lies perhaps in the tendency for wage costs to rise faster in the retailing sector than in the manufacturing sector because wage increases are not offset by productivity in retailing in the same way as they are in manufacturing. Although this is not built into the Cyert and March model, it is not inconceivable that such information would eventually filter through with a resultant (lagged) increase in mark-ups.

Behavioural rules and the firm

Papers by Baumol and Quandt (1964) and Day (1967) provide an alternative interpretation of behavioural rules and the firm to the interpretation provided by Cyert and March. Baumol and Quandt (1964) argue that, in view of the expense involved in say providing information, it is often undesirable to refine decision making and an approximate solution is adequate. Their paper proceeds to examine this point by testing the performance of certain rules of thumb by means of simulation techniques. Their findings were that a relatively simple rule of thumb performed well (in terms of the profits achieved); their analysis, however, was of a rather preliminary nature. Detailed discussion of behavioural rules and the firm is therefore confined to Day's papers in view of the fact that his work is more explicit on the relationship between the neoclassical theory of the firm and the behavioural theories.

Day argues that "a profound underlying unity" between "rational choice and behavioural principles" has escaped the notice of the behavioural theorists. His views on this point are probably worth stating in full:

"That such an intimate connection should have escaped the notice or been minimized by the proponents of the new approach is quite understandable. They have surely broadened by a considerable margin the operational understanding of the business concern and have contributed a substantial number of useful concepts and operational methods for analyzing behaviour. On the other hand, in its present state, behavioural theory fails to answer important questions formulated in optimizing theory and creates confusion in the theory of the firm in a wholly unnecessary way." (Day, 1967, p. 303.)

Day attempts to show this "unity" by means of a learning model constructed on behavioural lines which converges on the traditional rational or marginalist result.

Day assumes that a decision maker has one decision variable, output, x, and a single goal, which is satisfactory profit, Π. The decision maker does not know his profit function. He simply knows his past two decisions x_t, x_{t-1} and the corresponding profit figures Π_t, Π_{t-1}. Because the objective function is unknown to the decision maker he cannot maximize it. The rational approach in such a case is to adopt a learning process that improves goal fulfilment. The process adopted by Day's decision maker is based upon two principles:

1. Successful behaviour is to be repeated and unsuccessful behaviour is to be avoided.

2. Unsuccessful behaviour is to be restrained by greater caution if a repetition of it seems desirable again on some future occasion.

With the decision variable of the above problem the strategies can be summarized in the following table (which is reproduced from Day, 1967, p. 304).

Table 5.3

Past behaviour	Known consequences of past behaviour	
	Increase in profits	Decrease in profits
Expanded output	Expand output again	Contract output. Be more cautious in next expansion
Contracted output	Contract output again	Expand output. Be more cautious in next contraction

In addition, the decision maker requires a criterion of goal fulfilment. The criterion chosen is "when a past action leads to only a 'small' change in reward, the last output may be repeated". (Day, 1967, p. 304.) This follows because further changes can only produce insufficient payoff. (The possibilities seem to be either a small further increase in profits or even a decrease.) The "small change" referred to above Day calls the "satisficing parameter". Using this satisficing parameter and the other features of the model Day is able to show under the assumption that profit has a unique global maximum that as the decision maker chooses an arbitrary small value of his satisficing parameter so the model converges to the profit maximizing result of neoclassical economic theory, that MR = MC.

Day (in coauthorship with E. Herbert Tinney) has also produced a more complicated behavioural model of the firm in which the problem of decentralized decision making is taken into account. (See Day and Tinney, 1968, p. 598.) The firm (again operating in an unknown but deterministic environment) is divided into two decision making units, (i) the sales department and (ii) the engineering department. In line with his earlier paper, this paper was able to show that ". . . learning — tempered by caution in response to failure — can eventually gain the full amount of those rewards that would be possible from explicit optimizing behaviour. . . ." In addition, he was able to show that only very limited coordination between the departments was required to enable the optimum to be achieved.

The principal consequences of the work of Day and Tinney is to reveal an internal consistency between behavioural theory in a deterministic unknown environment and the neoclassical theory of the firm. In their own words they conclude that ". . . the competing theories of behavioural satisficing and or marginalism — at least in this context — are internally consistent and that their conclusions are separated by differences only in degree and not in kind." (Day and Tinney, 1968, p. 598.)

5.3 Quasi-neoclassical theories of the firm

Two further recent theories of the firm which emphasize motivation, organization, and decision making in the firm were developed by Williamson in the case of one of the theories, and by Crew, Rowley, and Jones-Lee in the case of the other theory. These theories are, because of their profit maximizing motivation, here termed quasi-neoclassical.

Williamson's M-form hypothesis

Oliver Williamson in his *Corporate Control and Business Behavior* (Williamson, 1970), demonstrates really the dramatic extension of his view of contemporary capitalism that has occurred since his earlier work on managerial discretion[16]. This later analysis is important in that it attempts to develop a further link between organizational theory and economics. He argues that the importance of his managerial discretion phenomenon depends upon the form of organization adopted by the firm. In particular, he argues that managerial discretion is applicable the "unitary" form of organization (U-form). However, innovations in organizational form have resulted in the development of the "multidivisional" form (M-form) which, Williamson argues, reduces the managerial discretion phenomenon and increases the applicability of the neoclassical profit maximizing assumption.

The U-form and the M-form of organization are set out in Fig. 5.4. From Fig. 5.4 it is clear that the U-form is preserved even in the case of the M-form at the lower levels of the organization hierarchy. This is because, as Williamson argues, "the U-form structure is the 'natural' way to organize multifunctional tasks". (Williamson, 1970, p. 110.) However, Williamson's argument is, that the U-form runs into problems of control as the firm expands. The firm is organized on functional lines and as it gets bigger it can only expand by adding further hierarchical levels of control, owing to the fact that spans of control are finite[17]. This results in difficulties in the transmission of data through the firm. This is exacerbated by the tendency for data to be summarized and interpreted at the various stages. With expansion the peak coordinator's (chief executive in diagram) capacity to deal with decisions is overloaded. This requires augmentation of his capacity. This is usually done by bringing in the heads of the functional division, thus giving them access to strategic as well as operating decisions. The way is thus clear for the managerial discretion that was described in section 5.1, where Williamson's earlier staff and emoluments model was examined. The interests of these functional executives is likely

Fig. 5.4

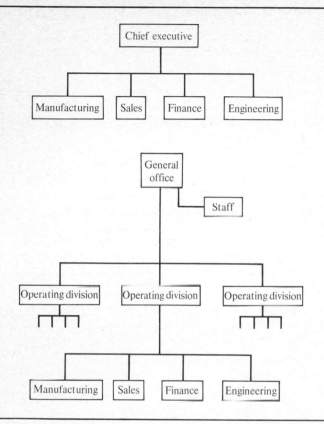

to be partisan and as such could be self-cancelling. However, they are likely to realize the benefits of consensus and they are likely to arrive at a consensus which might be modelled by the utility maximization framework of Williamson's managerial discretion models. The only control that can be exhibited in such a case would be that of the capital market (as it is assumed that the product market is not competitive).

The M-form as shown in the diagram has the following important features according to Williamson:

1. The responsibility for operating division is assigned to more or less self-contained operating divisions (these are U-forms).

2. The elite staff attached to the general office perform both advisory and auditing functions. These activities tend to secure greater control over operating division behaviour.

3.   The general office is concerned with strategic decisions, such as planning, appraisal, and control of the operating divisions.

4.   The separation of the general office from operations gives its executives the commitment to be concerned with overall performance and not just the affairs of one functional division.

5.   This point is most important and most subject to debate! To quote Williamson's own words, "The resulting structure displays both rationality and synergy: the whole is greater/more effective, more efficient than the sum of the parts." (Williamson, 1970, p. 121.)

The above features of the M-form, together with the evidence provided on the development of big business in the US by Chandler (1966), lead Williamson to formulate his "Multidivision form hypothesis" that: "the organization and operation of the large enterprise along the lines of the M-form favours goal pursuit and least-cost behaviour more nearly associated with the neoclassical profit maximization hypothesis than does the U-form organizational alternative". (Williamson, 1970, p. 134.)

The essential message of Williamson's recent contributions to the theory of the firm is that the form of organization influences firm behaviour and performance. This argument that the U-form is likely to support discretionary behaviour is an interesting addition to his theory. The M-form hypothesis, although has not been subject to any real formal testing, does represent a serious attempt at rehabilitation of neoclassical profit maximization and, as will be argued in Chapter 7, requires serious attention from economists.

The X-theory of the firm[18]

The X-theory also represents an attempt to revive profit maximization. In this one important respect, it is in agreement with the M-form hypothesis of Williamson. However, this is perhaps the only feature X-theory[19] and the M-form hypothesis have in common, because the X-theory shows how the objective of profit maximization can be consistent with X-efficiency[20].

Profit maximization is retained as the central objective in the X-theory of the firm on the supposition that this is the motivation of the equity shareholders and of their immediate representatives in whom the property rights are vested. With the separation between ownership and control, however, which is the hallmark of the modern corporation, clashes are likely between the objectives of these who own the equity and wish to maximize profits and those employed within the organization (management as well as shop floor) whose utility functions will rarely coincide with those of the equity shareholders. For labour, unlike capital, cannot be passively combined with other factors within the production process. Rather it is intent upon maximizing a utility function which is at odds with the utility function of the enterprise. If cooperation with the profit maximization objective is to be achieved in such circumstances, policing in one form or another will be required. In the absence of policing, X-inefficiency will be manifest within the organization even though the profit maximization objective prevails.

The most effective of all policing devices, from the viewpoint of surviving firms, is competition. For under strictly competitive conditions labour is constrained by market pressures into a policy of active coopera-tion, since the alternative to such cooperation very likely is the failure of the enterprise. This does not mean that competition will improve the quality of low-grade labour — to argue this is to commit "the fallacy that people can be different" — but it does imply that labour of whatever quality will be driven to cooperate to its best ability with the profit maximization objective in such conditions. From the viewpoint of the surviving firm, therefore, competition may be viewed as a costless policing mechanism. The transaction costs of bankruptcy ensure that it is not costless to society.

Once competition is diminished, however, and discretionary power exists the scope for labour non-cooperation arises and X-inefficiency will result in the absence of active policing. Non-cooperation may take many forms, as is evident from a cursory view of any organization, but a useful distinction may be made between active non-cooperation which results from goal conflicts within the organization (typified by the Williamson case in which management successfully subverts the institution to its own ends) and passive non-cooperation which results from labour's desire for the quiet life (typified by the shop-floor worker who retires to the toilet to read *Playboy*). It is not unreasonable to assume, with respect to both categories of labour non-cooperation, that X-inefficiency will prove to be a continuously increasing function of discretionary power (defined as the difference between maximum profit and the minimum profit required for survival).

In circumstances such as those described above, the equity interests within the firm will recognize that policing measures are required to moderate the incidence of X-inefficiency within the system. Typically, policing measures divide into the provision of monetary incentives for labour to cooperate with equity interests on the one hand (typified by stock-option schemes and profit-related bonuses for management and piece-rate systems and share-ownership schemes for shop floor labour) and by the provision of control devices on the other (typified by management consultant investigations and detailed systems of financial control to deal with management non-cooperation, and by work-study experts, foremen, gatekeepers, watchmen, and timekeepers to deal with shop floor inefficiency). Policing procedures such as those specified above themselves absorb economic resources and clearly it is unlikely in practice that policing expenditures will be applied to the point where labour cooperation is absolute. Policing costs are assumed to be independent of the firm's output rate and to manifest themselves as an overhead effect on total cost.

For purposes of the X-theory, the firm is assumed to maximize profit in terms of the following conditions:

Maximize $\pi = R - M - G$

where $\qquad \pi$ = profit

$\qquad\qquad R$ = revenue = PQ

$\qquad\qquad Q$ = output

$\qquad\qquad P$ = price = $P(Q)$

$\qquad\qquad M$ = costs (except policing costs) = $M(Q, G, \pi)$

$\qquad\qquad G$ = policing costs

$\qquad\qquad C$ = total costs = $M + G$

The optimal conditions are then given by

$$\frac{\partial R}{\partial Q} = \frac{\partial M}{\partial Q} \left(= \frac{\partial C}{\partial Q} \right) \qquad\qquad\qquad [5.8]$$

and

$$\frac{\partial M}{\partial G} = -1 \qquad\qquad\qquad [5.9]$$

Equation [5.8] states that marginal cost must be equated with marginal revenue, but it is worth re-emphasizing that this is not the familiar marginal cost of neoclassical analysis, which involves zero X-inefficiency. Equation [5.9] simply states that resources are devoted to policing labour until marginal policing costs are equated with marginal cost savings due to policing. In so far as X-inefficiency affects marginal cost the equilibrium output rate will be lower and the price higher than in the standard neoclassical solution.

Further restrictions, required for the comparative statics evaluation of the X-theory, concern the nature of demand, and the nature of the functional relationships between non-policing costs and policing costs, nonpolicing costs and profit, non-policing costs and output, and certain more complex cross-relationships. Only those relationships which are necessary for subsequent analysis are specified.

The demand curve is assumed to be linear and to take the general form

$$P = a - bQ \qquad [5.10]$$

where a is treated as a shift parameter. This simplifies subsequent analysis and facilitates the attainment of unambiguous qualitative predictions without over-restricting the theory.

Marginal non-policing costs are assumed to be positive and to be an increasing function of output rate, viz:

$$\frac{\partial M}{\partial Q} > 0 \quad \text{and} \quad \frac{\partial^2 M}{\partial Q^2} > 0 \qquad [5.11]$$

(These are the standard neoclassical assumptions.)

Non-policing costs are presumed, however, to be an increasing function of profit, since labour non-cooperation itself is an increasing function of discretionary power which is defined by reference to profit. Thus

$$\frac{\partial M}{\partial \pi} > 0 \qquad [5.12]$$

(This assumption is the essence of the X-theory.)

On the other hand, non-policing costs are a declining function of policing costs (which of course are designed to get rid of X-inefficiency). Thus

$$\frac{\partial M}{\partial G} < 0 \quad \text{and} \quad \frac{\partial^2 M}{\partial G^2} > 0 \qquad [5.13]$$

(Again, these assumptions go to the heart of the X-theory.)

Policing costs themselves are assumed to be independent of output rate and to feature as an overhead effect upon total cost. Thus

$$\frac{\partial G}{\partial Q} = 0 \qquad [5.14]$$

The nature of the cross-relationships between these several variables repays a close scrutiny, since they are of considerable importance in subsequent comparative statics analysis.

The first such relationship concerns the impact of a change in profit upon marginal non-policing costs. Inevitably, the impact will be a passive one, with the non-cooperation effects of rising profits rippling through the system largely, though not exclusively, as an overhead effect[21]. There will, nevertheless, be a detectable, though relatively small, positive effect upon marginal non-policing costs. Thus

$$\frac{\partial^2 M}{\partial Q \partial \pi} > 0 \qquad\qquad [5.15]$$

By contrast, changes in policing costs are likely to have a much more marked (though negative) effect upon marginal non-policing costs, since this is very much an active form of intervention and one likely to centre differential attention upon inefficiencies which affect marginal costs. Thus

$$\frac{\partial^2 M}{\partial Q \partial G} < 0 \qquad\qquad [5.16]$$

where

$$\left| \frac{\partial^2 M}{\partial Q \partial \pi} \right| \ll \left| \frac{\partial^2 M}{\partial Q \partial G} \right| \qquad\qquad [5.17]$$

Equally, changes in profits are likely to have a marked negative impact upon the rate of change of non-policing costs with respect to policing costs, intensifying the effectiveness of policing expenditure as profits (and potential labour non-cooperation) increase. Thus

$$\frac{\partial^2 M}{\partial G \partial \pi} < 0 \qquad\qquad [5.18]$$

where

$$\left| \frac{\partial^2 M}{\partial Q \partial \pi} \right| \ll \left| \frac{\partial^2 M}{\partial G \partial \pi} \right| \qquad\qquad [5.19]$$

This completes the formal specification of the model.

It is interesting to compare the qualitative predictions of the X-theory with the neoclassical and managerial discretion theories, i.e., response of output rate to
(i)   demand shift (a),
(ii) an increase in the rate of a proportional profits tax (t), and
(iii) the levying of a lump-sum tax ($\overline{T}$).
The comparison is outlined in Table 5.4.

Table 5.4 Comparative statics properties of X-theory compared with neoclassical and managerial discretion

| | Variable | Parameter | | |
		a	t	$\overline{T}$
Neoclassical	Q	+	0	0
Managerial discretion	Q	+	+ ?	−
X-theory	Q	+	−	−
	G	+	−	−

The output rate responses to demand shift displacement are identical for all three theories and provide no effective basis for discriminating between them. This is not the case, however, where displacement occurs via a change in the rate of the proportional profits tax or in a lump-sum tax. For neoclassical profit-maximization predicts that there will be no output response to "displacement" which bites only on profit treated as a residual as opposed to a contractual payment. By contrast, both the managerial discretion theory and the X-theory predict a non-zero response of output rate to taxes which bite on profits. Both theories predict a negative output rate response to a lump-sum tax, with the important inference for welfare economics that allocative effects can be expected from lump-sum taxes. The direction of output rate response to a change in the proportional profits tax is positive (questionably) in the managerial discretion theory but negative in the X-theory. This represents an important distinguishing characteristic and suggests a means possibly whereby the two theories can be empirically evaluated.

5.4 Critique

The "new" theories of the firm that have been examined here are important in that they reveal the implications for the theory of the firm when problems of motivation, and managerial decision-making are explicitly brought into the theory of the firm. They have produced several significantly different results which could have important implications for public policy (these will be discussed in Chapter 7). The theories, however, are still very much in their infancy, and are subject to a number of criticisms both at a theoretical and empirical level. While this section attempts to set out a few such criticisms it should not detract from the substantial, actual and potential contribution of these theories.

All the theories considered here have to be yet subjected to extensive empirical testing. A brief comment on empirical testing will therefore follow the critique of the theories on theoretical grounds. Perhaps the most significant criticism of the Baumol theory of sales maximization has been made by Rosenberg (1971). It is Baumol's use of a constraint in the objective function which Rosenberg criticises. By postulating that the firm seeks to maximize revenue subject to a profit constraint, Baumol implies

Fig. 5.5

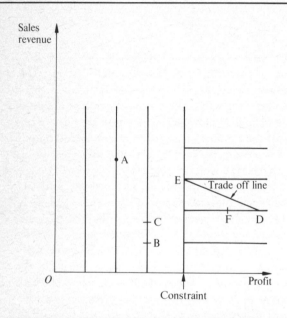

that the firm orders each combination of profit and sales in a lexico-graphic[22] manner, as shown in Fig. 5.5 (which is reproduced from Rosenberg, 1971, p. 208). Thus the firm orders combinations as follows:

1. For any two combinations, both having profits below the constraint, the one with the larger profit will be preferred (B is preferable to A) regardless of sales. Similarly, if both have the same profit the one with the higher sales is preferred (i.e., C is preferred to B).

2. For any two combinations, both having profits equal to or greater than the constraint the outcome with the greater sales revenue is preferred (E preferred to D). If both have the same sales the one with larger profits is preferred (D preferred to F).

Because Baumol's model assumes that profit will always be converted into revenue through advertising, it follows that profit will always be converted into advertising to increase sales, so long as profit exceeds the constraint. Thus if the firm can attain a position like D in Fig. 5.5 by profit maximizing, it will always move along a tradeoff line like DE until it hits the profit constraint. Irrespective of how small the increase in sales is relative to profit the firm will make this trade. This implies a distinctly unusual type of marginal rate of substitution (MRS) of sales for profit. It is infinite so long as profit exceeds the constraint, and zero when it is below the constraint. Rosenberg argues, "While such an ordering is conceptually possible there does not seem any economic rationale for supposing that such a strong and unstable pattern should exist." (Rosenberg, 1971, p. 209.) Indeed the approach adopted by Williamson, which implies more conventional MRS between the variables in the utility function, seems to be more fruitful.

Although Rosenberg's criticism represents a serious fundamental criticism of the form of Baumol's sales revenue maximizing model, it should not be regarded as a fundamental criticism of Baumol's message. Clearly sales have very special importance for firms and Baumol has provided an important contribution by showing that the kind of effects that pursuit of sales might have for the behaviour of firms. The Cyert and March behavioural theory might be criticized most severely on the grounds that it is questionable whether it is a theory at all. Normally a theory is expected to do more than deal with an individual case. Even with the extensions made by Baumol and Stewart it is still not clear that Cyert and March have not done much more than modelled particular cases rather successfully. Despite such criticisms of behavioural theory, it is clear that it has made a major contribution in widening the perspective of economists by introducing them to organizational theory and encouraging them to explore the role of rules of thumb. This task has been well attempted by Day.

There are several general failings applicable to most of the new theories of the firm. They have not yet been developed for purposes of the theory of market structures. It is assumed that the firm concerned are usually oligopolists. However, no theory of oligopoly comparable to the profit maximizing models of oligopoly as discussed in Chapter 4 has been developed.

On the question of empirical testing, there is still considerable scope for more formal examination of the empirical significance of the theories. Almost all the theories have been subject to some testing. For example, Williamson (1967) has tested his own results himself; Newbould (1970) has attempted to try and assess the significance of Marris's contribution on the valuation ratio and takeovers; similarly, Singh (1971) in a wider ranging study has examined related problems. The Williamson M-form hypothesis is potentially one of the most important recent contributions to the theory of the firm, providing as it does the basis for determining the applicability of the theory of the firm according to the organizational form of the enterprise. It raises a number of interesting questions about the scale and efficiency of firms. For example, are M-form companies really more X-efficient? Does the synergy really exist? Is not the X-theory rather than the neoclassical profit maximizing theory more relevant in the context of the M-form?

Appendix on comparative statics and X-theory[1]

The purpose of this appendix is to provide a formal derivation of the comparative statics properties of the "X-theory" model. The standard technique of total differentiation of the first-order conditions for profit maximization is employed. It is provided to assist the reader in answering problems on comparative statics, viz. Exercises 1 and 2.

The X-theory yields a profit function of the form

$$\pi = [(a - bQ)Q - M(Q, G, \pi) - G](1 - t) - T \tag{1'}$$

The effects of both a proportional-profits tax and a lump-sum tax on the behaviour of the firm were shown in Table 5.4. They are now derived in detail.

First-order conditions for profit maximization are

$$\frac{\partial \pi}{\partial Q} = \frac{\partial \pi}{\partial G} = 0 \tag{2'}$$

But, from [1']

$$\frac{\partial \pi}{\partial Q} = \left[a - 2bQ - \frac{\partial M}{\partial Q} - \frac{\partial M}{\partial \pi} \cdot \frac{\partial \pi}{\partial Q} \right] (1 - t) \tag{3'}$$

or, rearranging [3'],

$$\frac{\partial \pi}{\partial Q} = \frac{\left(a - 2bQ - \dfrac{\partial M}{\partial Q} \right)}{\left(\dfrac{1}{1 - t} + \dfrac{\partial M}{\partial \pi} \right)} \tag{4'}$$

Also from [1']

$$\frac{\partial \pi}{\partial G} = \left[-\frac{\partial M}{\partial G} - \frac{\partial M}{\partial \pi} \cdot \frac{\partial \pi}{\partial G} - 1 \right] (1 - t) \tag{5'}$$

or, rearranging [5']

$$\frac{\partial \pi}{\partial G} = \frac{\left(-\dfrac{\partial M}{\partial G} - 1\right)}{\left(\dfrac{1}{1-t} + \dfrac{\partial M}{\partial \pi}\right)} \tag{6'}$$

Hence, from [2'], [4'] and [6'] the first-order conditions for profit maximization are given by[2]

$$a - 2nQ - \frac{\partial M}{\partial Q} = 0 \tag{7'}$$

$$\frac{\partial M}{\partial G} + 1 = 0 \tag{8'}$$

Second-order conditions for profit maximization are

$$\frac{\partial^2 \pi}{\partial Q^2} < 0 \tag{9'}$$

and

$$\begin{vmatrix} \dfrac{\partial^2 \pi}{\partial Q^2} & \dfrac{\partial^2 \pi}{\partial Q \partial G} \\[2ex] \dfrac{\partial^2 \pi}{\partial G \partial Q} & \dfrac{\partial^2 \pi}{\partial G^2} \end{vmatrix} > 0 \tag{10'}$$

From [4'] and [7'], [9'] may be written as

$$\frac{\left(-2b - \dfrac{\partial^2 M}{\partial Q^2}\right)}{\left(\dfrac{1}{1-t} + \dfrac{\partial M}{\partial \pi}\right)} < 0 \tag{11'}$$

So that for $b > 0$, $0 < t < 1$, $(\partial M/\partial \pi) > 0$ and $(\partial^2 M/\partial Q^2) > 0$ [11'] is satisfied.

From [4'], [6'], [7'] and [8'] we may write [10'] as

$$\frac{1}{\left(\dfrac{1}{1-t} + \dfrac{\partial M}{\partial \pi}\right)^2} \left\{ \left(2b + \frac{\partial^2 M}{\partial Q^2}\right) \left(\frac{\partial^2 M}{\partial G^2}\right) - \left(\frac{\partial^2 M}{\partial Q \partial G}\right)^2 \right\} > 0 \tag{12'}$$

The relative magnitudes of $\partial^2 M/\partial Q^2$, $\partial^2 M/\partial G^2$ and $\partial^2 M/\partial Q\partial G$ must therefore be such as to satisfy [12'] in order that the second-order conditions for profit maximization should be fulfilled.

Now consider a profit maximizing firm producing and policing at positive finite rates: Q and G will be such as to satisfy [7'] and [8']. Suppose now that a change occurs in some or all of the parameters of the problem. If, after the change in the parameters, the firm continues to produce and police at positive finite rates then the changed values of Q and G will also satisfy [7'] and [8'].

Changes in parameters and decision variables will, under these conditions, satisfy the total differentials of [7'] and [8'], which are given by

$$\mathrm{d}a - 2b\,\mathrm{d}Q - 2Q\,\mathrm{d}b - \frac{\partial^2 M}{\partial Q^2}\,\mathrm{d}Q - \frac{\partial^2 M}{\partial Q\partial G}\,\mathrm{d}G - \frac{\partial^2 M}{\partial Q\partial \pi}\,\mathrm{d}\pi = 0 \qquad [13']$$

$$\frac{\partial^2 M}{\partial G^2}\,\mathrm{d}G + \frac{\partial^2 M}{\partial G\partial Q}\,\mathrm{d}Q + \frac{\partial^2 M}{\partial G\partial \pi}\,\mathrm{d}\pi = 0 \qquad [14']$$

But, from [1'] it follows that

$$\mathrm{d}\pi = \left[a\,\mathrm{d}Q + Q\,\mathrm{d}a - 2bQ\,\mathrm{d}Q - Q^2\,\mathrm{d}b - \frac{\partial M}{\partial Q}\,\mathrm{d}Q - \right.$$

$$\left. - \frac{\partial M}{\partial G}\,\mathrm{d}G - \frac{\partial M}{\partial \pi}\,\mathrm{d}\pi - \mathrm{d}G \right] (1 - t) - \theta\,\mathrm{d}t - \mathrm{d}T \quad [15']$$

where θ is defined as

$$\theta = (a - bQ)Q - M(Q, G, \pi) - G$$

Rearranging [15']

$$\mathrm{d}\pi = \frac{1}{\phi}\left[a\,\mathrm{d}Q + Q\,\mathrm{d}a - 2bQ\,\mathrm{d}Q - Q^2\,\mathrm{d}b - \frac{\partial M}{\partial Q}\,\mathrm{d}Q - \frac{\partial M}{\partial G}\,\mathrm{d}G - \mathrm{d}G \right]$$

$$- \frac{\theta\,\mathrm{d}t}{(1 - t)\phi} - \frac{\mathrm{d}T}{(1 - t)\phi} \qquad [16']$$

where ϕ is defined as

$$\phi = \frac{1}{1 - t} + \frac{\partial M}{\partial \pi}$$

Hence, from [13'], [14'] and [16'],

$$\left\{-2b - \frac{\partial^2 M}{\partial Q^2} - \frac{\partial^2 M}{\partial Q \partial \pi} \frac{1}{\phi}\left[a - 2bQ - \frac{\partial M}{\partial Q}\right]\right\} dQ +$$

$$+ \left\{-\frac{\partial^2 M}{\partial Q \partial G} - \frac{\partial^2 M}{\partial Q \partial \pi} \frac{1}{\phi}\left[-\frac{\partial M}{\partial G} - 1\right]\right\} dG$$

$$= -da + 2Q\, db + \frac{\partial^2 M}{\partial Q \partial \pi} \frac{1}{\phi}\left\{Q\, da - Q^2\, db - \right.$$

$$\left. - \frac{\theta \cdot}{(1 - \iota)}\, dt - \frac{dT}{(1 - t)}\right\} \tag{17'}$$

$$\left\{\frac{\partial^2 M}{\partial G \partial Q} + \frac{\partial^2 M}{\partial G \partial \pi} \frac{1}{\phi}\left[a - 2bQ - \frac{\partial M}{\partial Q}\right]\right\} dQ +$$

$$+ \left\{\frac{\partial^2 M}{\partial G^2} + \frac{\partial^2 M}{\partial G \partial \pi} \frac{1}{\phi}\left[-\frac{\partial M}{\partial G} - 1\right]\right\} dG$$

$$= -\frac{\partial^2 M}{\partial G \partial \pi} \frac{1}{\phi}\left\{Q\, da - Q^2\, db - \frac{\theta}{(1 - t)}\, dt - \frac{dT}{(1 - t)}\right\} \tag{18'}$$

However, notice that, from [7'] and [8'], all expressions within square brackets in [17'] and [18'] are zero. Employing this simplification and writing [17'] and [18'] in matrix form it follows that

$$\begin{bmatrix} \left(-2b - \dfrac{\partial^2 M}{\partial Q^2}\right) - \dfrac{\partial^2 M}{\partial Q \partial G} \\[2ex] \dfrac{\partial^2 M}{\partial G \partial Q} \quad \dfrac{\partial^2 M}{\partial G^2} \end{bmatrix} \begin{bmatrix} dQ \\[2ex] dG \end{bmatrix}$$

$$= \begin{bmatrix} -da + 2Q\, db + \dfrac{\partial^2 M}{\partial Q \partial \pi} \dfrac{1}{\phi}\left\{Q\, da - Q^2\, db - \dfrac{\theta\, dt}{(1 - t)} - \dfrac{dT}{(1 - t)}\right\} \\[3ex] -\dfrac{\partial^2 M}{\partial G \partial \pi} \dfrac{1}{\phi}\left\{Q\, da - Q^2\, db - \dfrac{\theta}{(1 - t)}\, dt - \dfrac{dT}{(1 - t)}\right\} \end{bmatrix}$$

$$\tag{19'}$$

Now in order to examine the effect of a *ceteris paribus* increase in the lump-sum tax set $dT > 0$ and $da = db = dt = 0$. Then from [19'] by matrix inversion[3], the following are derived:

$$dQ = \frac{dT}{|D|} \left\{ -\frac{\partial^2 M}{\partial G^2} \frac{\partial^2 M}{\partial Q \partial \pi} \cdot \frac{1}{\phi} \frac{1}{(1-t)} + \frac{\partial^2 M}{\partial Q \partial G} \frac{\partial^2 M}{\partial G \partial \pi} \frac{1}{\phi} \frac{1}{(1-t)} \right\} \quad [20']$$

$$dG = \frac{dT}{|D|} \left\{ \frac{\partial^2 M}{\partial G \partial Q} \frac{\partial^2 M}{\partial Q \partial \pi} \cdot \frac{1}{\phi} \frac{1}{(1-t)} - \left(2b + \frac{\partial^2 M}{\partial Q^2} \right) \frac{\partial^2 M}{\partial G \partial \pi} \frac{1}{\phi} \frac{1}{(1-t)} \right\} \quad [21']$$

where $|D|$ is the determinant of the coefficient matrix on the left-hand side of [19'] and is given by

$$|D| = -\left(2b + \frac{\partial^2 M}{\partial Q^2} \right) \frac{\partial^2 M}{\partial G^2} + \left(\frac{\partial^2 M}{\partial Q \partial G} \right)^2 \quad [22']$$

Hence, if second-order conditions for profit maximization are fulfilled then from [12']

$$|D| < 0 \quad [23']$$

Now restrictions have already been placed upon the signs of the second partial derivations of M with respect to its arguments: it will be recalled that these were

$$\frac{\partial^2 M}{\partial Q^2} > 0, \quad \frac{\partial^2 M}{\partial G^2} > 0, \quad \frac{\partial^2 M}{\partial Q \partial G} < 0, \quad \frac{\partial^2 M}{\partial Q \partial \pi} > 0, \quad \frac{\partial^2 M}{\partial G \partial \pi} < 0.$$

It has also been argued that

$$\left| \frac{\partial^2 M}{\partial Q \partial \pi} \right| \ll \left| \frac{\partial^2 M}{\partial Q \partial G} \right| \quad \text{and} \quad \left| \frac{\partial^2 M}{\partial Q \partial \pi} \right| \ll \left| \frac{\partial^2 M}{\partial G \partial \pi} \right|.$$

With these restrictions on the signs and magnitudes of the second partial derivatives of M and noting that for $0 < t < 1$ and $\partial M / \partial \pi > 0$ it follows that (by definition) $\phi > 0$; it follows from [20'] that if $dT > 0$ then $dQ < 0$ and from [21'] that if $dT > 0$ then $dG < 0$. A *ceteris paribus* increase in the lump sum tax therefore causes both output and policing expenditure to be reduced.

Similarly by setting $dt > 0$ and $da = db = dT = 0$, and noting that for pre-tax profit positive we have (by definition) $\theta > 0$, it can be shown that a *ceteris paribus* increase in the rate of the proportional profits tax also causes both output and policing expenditure to be reduced.

Finally, consider a *ceteris paribus* increase in the demand shift parameter a. Setting $da > 0$ and $db = dt = dT = 0$ and solving [19'] by matrix invesion the following are derived:

$$dQ = \frac{da}{|D|} \left\{ \frac{\partial^2 M}{\partial G^2} \left(-1 + \frac{\partial^2 M}{\partial Q \partial \pi} \cdot \frac{Q}{\phi} \right) - \frac{\partial^2 M}{\partial Q \partial G} \cdot \frac{\partial^2 M}{\partial G \partial \pi} \frac{Q}{\phi} \right\} \quad [24']$$

$$dG = \frac{da}{|D|} \left\{ -\frac{\partial^2 M}{\partial G \partial Q} \left(-1 + \frac{\partial^2 M}{\partial Q \partial \pi} \frac{Q}{\phi} \right) + \left(2b + \frac{\partial^2 M}{\partial Q^2} \right) \frac{\partial^2 M}{\partial G \partial \pi} \frac{Q}{\phi} \right\} \quad [25']$$

The restrictions on the signs and magnitudes of the second partial derivatives of M therefore imply that (for $\phi > 0$) $da > 0$ gives $dQ > 0$ and $dG > 0$. A *ceteris paribus* increase in the demand shift parameter therefore causes both output and policing expenditure to increase.

Exercises — 5

1. Derive the comparative statics properties of Williamson's staff model, using Williamson's notation, viz. $Z_i = X, S, \alpha_k = E, t, \overline{T}$, and Williamson's assumptions regarding the sign of $\dfrac{\partial^2 U}{\partial z_i \partial \alpha_k}$ which is given below.

	E	t	$\overline{T}$
X	+	0	0
S	+	+ ?	−

Hint: Differentiate the first-order conditions, $\dfrac{\partial U}{\partial z_i} = 0$, with respect to α_l, to give, by the function of a function rule,

$$\sum_{j=1}^{2} \frac{\partial^2 U}{\partial z_i \partial z_j} \cdot \frac{\partial z_j}{\partial \alpha_k} + \frac{\partial^2 U}{\partial z_i \partial \alpha_k} = 0$$

Write in matrix form and solve for $\dfrac{\partial z_1}{\partial \alpha_1}, \dfrac{\partial z_1}{\partial \alpha_2}$, using Cramer's rule. Assume that $\dfrac{\partial^2 U}{\partial z_i \partial z_j}$ as follows:

$$\left\| \begin{matrix} - & + \\ + & - \end{matrix} \right\|$$

2.   Show that the X-theory predicts that an increase in a proportional-profits tax will cause the firm to reduce output and policing expenditure.

3.   Show that the minimum profit constraint will always be binding on the assumption that the marginal revenue of advertising is positive. First solve the following problem:

Maximize revenue = R

Subject to $R - VC - WA \geqslant K$

Where $C = C(x) =$ total cost and $A =$ advertising expenditure, K is the required minimum profit; V and W are constants (assumed positive).

4.   A revenue maximizing firm (who happens to be a monopolist) requires a profit of at least 1,000. His demand and cost functions are given by $p = 300 - q$ and TC $= 600 + 5q + 10q^2$. How do his output, price, and profit compare with the equivalent quantities under profit maximizing monopoly?

Notes

1.   For a discussion of this and a general introduction to managerial and other theories of the firm see Machlup (1967).

2.   Several organization theorists have noted this tendency of large organizations. For example, Thompson (1961, p. 24) argues that ". . . the modern organization is a prolific generator of anxiety and insecurity. *It would be difficult to imagine a more efficient one.*" (Emphasis added.)

3.   Of course to the extent that competition is severe, e.g., through freedom of entry, there may be little difference between these two bounds.

4. U_1 is the first partial of the utility function with respect to S; U_2 is the first partial with respect to M, and U_3 is the first partial with respect to $(1 - t)(R - C - S - M - \bar{T}) - \Pi_0$.

5.   This does not mean that output is the same as that of a profit maximizing firm because of the effect of S on P and, from equation [5.5], the fact that S is greater than under profit maximization.

6. The reader is encouraged to check that he understands how such results are derived by working Exercise 1 at the end of this chapter. Actually, Exercise 1 requires the reader to produce comparative statics properties of the Williamson staff model because comparative statics properties cannot be derived for the staff and emoluments model in the usual way (see Williamson (1967, pp. 54, 66–71)). However, the staff model, being a simpler mode, can be solved without problems.

7. Actually Baumol's argument relies on the addition of an advertising variable. By assuming, not unreasonably, that marginal revenue of advertising is positive he can easily show that $\lambda > 0$ and therefore that the constraint is binding. The reader is encouraged to develop this point in Exercise 3 at the end of this chapter.

8. As Baumol notes, they could just as easily represent sales in two different markets, or two different products.

9. No attempt is going to be made to summarize Marris's introductory argument beyond this, or to refer to the underlying literature used by Marris to support his arguments as he has fully referenced this. One point, however, that will be taken up later is the question of security.

10. While Marris does not formally incorporate this constraint into the objective function in the sense that Baumol does, he appears to regard it in the same way as Baumol's profit constraint. For example, he states (Marris, 1964, p. 45), "For the first part of the book, however (more precisely, up to p. 254) we continue to treat the valuation ratio as a constraint."

11. The interest in the internal organization of firms by economists was certainly not common. Adam Smith, however, recognized the importance of the problem, when he saw that monopoly had other perhaps more serious consequences in addition to the textbook allocative inefficiency arising from fixing a price in excess of marginal cost. He viewed monopoly as enabling "the company to support the negligence, profusion, and malversation of their own servants, whose disorderly conduct seldom allows the company to exceed the ordinary rate of profit in trades which are altogether free." (Smith, 1952, p. 330.) J. R. Hicks (1935) had also made a similar point in the 1930s but it was not immediately taken up.

12. Leibenstein's first paper on this subject appeared in 1966 and was followed by papers by Comanor and Leibenstein (1969), Crew and

Rowley (1971), which indicated the nature of the problem. For a discussion of the public policy implications of X-inefficiency and the theory of the firm see Chapter 7.

13. Comanor and Leibenstein (1969, p. 304) explain the situation as follows:

"In estimating the loss from monopoly, it has been common to assume that inputs are used as efficiently as in competitive markets. The presumed reason for this assumption is that firms have a clear interest in minimizing costs per unit of output. While the 'carrot' of greater profits may well be a major determinant of firm behaviour, the competitive 'stick' may be equally important, and to this extent monopoly will affect costs as well as prices."

Any higher costs arising are said to stem from X-inefficiency.

14. Alchian, 1950, p. 212. Tintner produced several papers in this area (1941a, 1941b, 1942).

15. Baumol and Stewart (1971) discuss these and other problems in an interesting evaluation of behavioural theories which includes non-economic aspects.

16. He, in fact, shows how these ideas are a development of his earlier work, and how they follow from developments in capitalism which have been, if anything, accelerating in the period since publication of his earlier work.

17. Williamson has developed this argument in Williamson (1967) which is reproduced in modified form in Chapter 2 of his book (1970).

18. This sub-section is based upon Crew, Jones-Lee, and Rowley (1971).

19. Attempts to explain how X-inefficiency arises in the context of the theory of the firm have originated from Leibenstein (1969, 1973).

20. As mentioned in note 12, the neoclassical theory of monopoly, for example, excludes the possibility of X-inefficiency. When costs are not minimized for a given level of output profits are automatically not maximized. Thus X-inefficiency is logically excluded.

21. That is they mainly affect fixed costs. For a discussion of overhead effects see Crew and Rowley (1971a).

22. For vectors X and Y, X is lexicographically greater than Y if $x_1 > y_1$ or $x_1 = y_1$ and $x_2 > y_2$, or $x_1 = y_1$, $x_2 = y_2, \ldots, x_p = y_p$, and $x_{p+1} > y_{p+1}$.

Notes to appendix

1. This is reproduced in slightly modified form Crew, Jones-Lee, and Rowley (1971).

2. Notice that $[7']$ requires the marginal revenue be equal to the first partial derivative of M with respect to Q. This follows from requiring marginal revenue to be equal to the total rate of change of M with respect to Q including a "feed-back" effect through π, i.e.,

$$a - 2bQ - \frac{\partial M}{\partial Q} - \frac{\partial M}{\partial \pi} \cdot \frac{\partial \pi}{\partial Q} = 0,$$

and noting that at the maximum value of π, $\partial \pi / \partial Q = 0$ so that the feedback effect vanishes!

3. Williamson's analysis explicitly employs Cramer's rule at this stage.

6

General equilibrium, growth, stochastic demand and the firm

This chapter is concerned with the examination of some remaining areas of interest in the theory of the firm. While all the topics, general equilibrium, growth, and uncertainty are important, they are for the most part new and highly complex areas of study and some of the results are therefore rather provisional and have not yet been integrated into the theory of the firm. One aim of this chapter is therefore to show the significance of such complex developments for the theory of the firm. Section 6.1 will deal with general equilibrium and the firm. This is a difficult subject whose significance for the theory of the firm has yet to be determined. What follows therefore attempts to state some of the major issues involved. Section 6.2 will examine some problems of the growth of firms. Section 6.3 will extend the earlier discussion in the context of the behavioural theory of the firm to a somewhat more formal analysis of uncertainty, and its relation to the theory of the firm. Section 6.4 will be concerned with some conclusions, and with discussion of the scope for further development in the theory of the firm in these developing areas of study.

6.1 General equilibrium analysis
The development of the first five chapters of this book has been concerned with the individual firm in the context of the market where it sells its output. This section is concerned with an examination of how the firm fits in with all the other economic units forming the economy as a whole. The advances in general equilibrium theory over the past twenty-five years have been so considerable that it might give a false impression of modern economics if the subject was ignored in a book on the theory of the firm[1]. These developments have been so substantial and so technical that it

would be impossible to do justice to them in a short section. This section will aim therefore only at providing an elementary view of the subject, leaving the reader interested in developing the technical aspects to turn to the variety of books now available[2]. A brief discussion of the nature of general equilibrium will be followed by a discussion of a number of questions still unanswered.

The analysis employed so far has been solely concerned with so-called partial equilibrium models. The firm is one component in the economy and its behaviour has been analysed on its own without reference to the behaviour of the rest of the economy. The familiar approach of *ceteris paribus* has been employed. To the extent that firms meet consumers in markets, one form of interaction of the firm with other economic agents has been considered. The general equilibrium approach, in contrast to the above approach, examines the individual functioning of the parts, and their mutual conditioning, to generate a picture of the whole. The point above general equilibrium analysis is that all the prices and quantities must be determined together. It is not possible to find one price and then another. Thus in general equilibrium the simultaneous determination of all prices and quantities occurs. This raises interesting questions, such as why should the behaviour of consumers who independently maximize utility, and firms who independently maximize their profits, combine in such a way that equilibrium is attained in every market?[3]

Like Macaulay's schoolboy, every economist knows that a major preoccupation of general equilibrium theorists was counting equations and unknowns. This followed from the fact that prices and quantities had to be simultaneously determined. So the nature of the system of equations in the general equilibrium system was of obvious interest. The contribution of Walras (1954) was to show that the system had an identical number of equations and unknowns. The problem arose from the fact that it is only relative prices that matter in the general equilibrium system. The procedure was to consider a system with n prices. Since it is *relative* prices that are under consideration, $n - 1$ of the prices are measured in terms of the price of the nth good, where the nth good is the so-called numerative. However, this results in an excess of equations over variables. The problem was resolved by Walras who showed that one of these equations could be eliminated[4].

Walras' law is very famous and very important in the development of general equilibrium theory. However, it does not provide an assurance of the existence of an equilibrium solution. Systems may have many mathematical solutions or no solution. The existence of a mathematical solution may not be adequate because it violates the (implicit) bounds placed upon variables by economics. For example, prices, output levels, and input quantities are normally required to be non-negative. Thus any mathematical solution containing negative consumption levels is meaningless. The modern approach to general equilibrium provides a solution to these kinds of problems at a general level. They show the existence of equilibrium solutions for all multi-market general equilibrium systems which satisfy certain general assumptions. In particular, it can be proved using advanced mathematics including topology that an equilibrium exists for a perfectly competitive economy for most initial endowments of wealth[5], as long as there are no indivisibilities or increasing returns.

The contribution of Arrow (1971)[6] has been to extend general equilibrium analysis. In particular, he has provided an existence proof for the case of an economy with a monopolistically competitive sector (and a perfectly competitive sector) with increasing returns and downward-sloping demand curves. This section will be concerned with discussion of the implications of Arrow's analysis for the theory of the firm in general equilibrium. To this end Archibald's discussion of Arrow's paper (Archibald, 1971) should be examined for more detail.

While Arrow's paper extended the previous work on monopolistic competition (Negishi, 1960—61) to cases of non-convex production possibility sets there are a number of omissions from the analysis. For example, there is no scope for free entry which was an important aspect of Chamberlin's model (see Chapter 4). Arrow also assumes that prices charged by monopolistic firms are continuous functions of other prices and other production and consumption decisions. As Arrow himself recognizes, "The assumption of continuity may be strong nevertheless; in effect it denies the role of increasing returns as a barrier to entry." (Arrow, 1971, p. 97.) Arrow's analysis also ignores any question of power of firms and rivalry between firms. It thus does not deal with oligopoly problems. Thus it would appear that while substantial advances have been made in the theory of general equilibrium a lot of problems remain regarding the firm in general equilibrium.

6.2   Growth and the firm

In Chapter 5 some consideration was given to the nature of modern corporations and the reason why, according to Marris, firms (managers) might be interested in growth and might be motivated towards achieving it. Certainly growth is a very important concern of businessmen in the same way as it is a concern of the government in relation to the whole economy. Indeed economists have been concerned for many years with the development of macroeconomic growth models, and considerations of optimal growth. The interest by economists in growth at the firm has been much more recent beginning with work on the growth of the firm by Penrose (1959). Marris (1964) was next to make a major contribution in this area followed by J. H. Williamson (1966). Further consideration was given to problems of growth and the firm by Marris and Solow in Marris (1971). The model developed by Solow is important for its ability not only to provide a summary and critique of the essential arguments of Marris and Williamson but also for its ability to answer some important questions about the implications of growth. The principal questions that arise about growth theories of the firm are of the "so what?" variety. In other words, it is quite conceivable that growth models based on all sorts of motivation produced the same effects as do models based upon say profit maximization or its equivalent in growth theory, viz. present value of the firm (see below).

The growth models developed by Marris, Williamson, and Solow are all of the so-called "steady-state" variety. This means that the firm chooses once and for all its constant rate of growth at which it grows for ever. This simplifying assumption enables growth to be studied with the familiar maximizing framework of calculus[7].

Solow symbolizes the growth rate of the firm as g. (For simplicity, most of Solow's original notation will be retained.) All prices are assumed to be constant, and the economy itself is assumed to have growth at g_0 which is always greater than g. (Otherwise the firm would eventually take over the whole economy.) The complete list of variables employed using Solow's notation is given below:

g = constant growth rate of firm (output, capital assets, employment)

g_0 = constant growth rate of economy where $g_0 > g$

m = unit cost of capital

f = depreciation rate per unit of time

b = number of units of output produced by unit of capital

a = variable costs per unit of *capital*

n = elasticity of demand = constant

$S(g)$ = selling costs to achieve growth in sales of g expressed as a fraction of sales revenue[8]

$T(g) = 1 - S(g)$

i = discount rate. (The appropriate rate, given the pure rate of interest, takes into account such factors as the riskiness of the type of business which the firm is in.)

Q = output

p = price = $Q^{-1/n}$ (since n is constant elasticity)

$\theta \quad = 1 - 1/n$

$K \quad$ = the firm's stock of capital

Solow's approach is to derive an expression for the market value of the firm and then compare conventional motivation with Marris and J. H. Williamson's assumptions regarding motivation of the firm. Before setting out this expression for value of the firm it is necessary to make a few more assumptions and comment further on the above list of variables. Throughout constant returns to scale are employed. Thus current costs per unit of capital are summarized by a or $\dfrac{a}{b}$ per unit of output. The value of the firm is the present value of the dividend stream discounted at i. In such circumstances the value of the firm is independent of its financial structure. (See Modigliani and Miller, 1961.)

Hence it is assumed that all growth is financed entirely out of retained earnings.

The value of the firm (V) is therefore given by

$$V = \int_0^\infty [T(g)b^\theta K^\theta - (a + m(f + g))K]\, e^{(g-i)t}\, dt$$

$$= \left[\frac{[T(g)b^\theta K^\theta - (a + m(f+g))K]e^{(g-i)t}}{g - i} \right]_0^\infty$$

$$= \frac{T(g)b^\theta K^\theta - (a + m(f + g))K}{i - g} \qquad [6.1]$$

It is easily seen how expression [6.1] is derived. The right-hand side of the first line is the present value of revenues minus costs including all expenditure on investment. As Revenue $= pQ\, e^{gt} = Q^\theta\, e^{gt}$ (recall $p = Q^{-1/n}$, and $\theta = 1-1/n$), it follows that revenue less selling costs can be written as $T(g)b^\theta K^\theta\, e^{gt}$ (obviously $Q = bK$ because b is output produced from a unit of capital). All other costs including current costs (which comprise depreciation, f, and variable costs, a, per unit) amount to $(a + mf)K\, e^{gt}$. Finally, it is necessary to take into account investment in new capital which is financed entirely out of retained earnings. As the firm is growing at rate g, the cost of net investment in new capital is given by $mgK\, e^{gt}$. Thus the total of current costs and the costs of net investment amounts to $[a + m(f + g)]K\, e^{gt}$. This is deducted from revenue (derived above) and discounted (this simply involves multiplying by e^{-it}) to give V. It should, of course, be noted that i is assumed to be greater than g, or as Solow puts it "... by just assuming that $T(g)$ falls to zero for some g less than i". (p. 323.)

Fig. 6.1

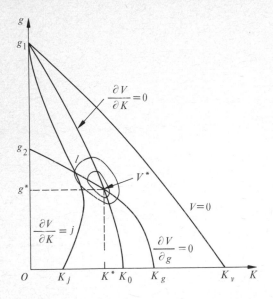

The valuation function [6.1] can be illustrated graphically (as shown in Fig. 6.1) by means of the familiar analysis of plotting contours. On the horizontal axis K is plotted; on the vertical axis g is plotted. A number of contours are shown. These are "iso-valuation" curves each one corresponding to a particular level of V. The locus of points where $V = 0$ is given by Og_1K_v. The points actually on the vertical axis are obvious since they consist of $K = 0$. The rest of the locus g_1K_v is derived by setting $V = 0$ and then solving for K. This curve leaves the vertical axis at g_1 where $T(g_1) = 0$ and falls steadily to cut the horizontal axis at K_v, i.e.,

$$K = \left(\frac{T(g)b^\theta}{a + m(f + g)} \right)^n \qquad [6.2]^9$$

[6.2] cuts the horizontal axis at K_v which is obtained by inserting $T(0)$ in [6.2]. Thus V is positive inside the locus $K_v g_1$.

The other point of interest is where V attains a maximum. This occurs at $\frac{\partial V}{\partial K} = 0$ and $\frac{\partial V}{\partial g} = 0$.

Partially differentiating V with respect to K and g yields

$$\frac{\partial V}{\partial K} = \frac{\theta T(g)b^\theta K^{\theta-1} - a - m(f + g)}{i - g} \qquad [6.3]$$

$$\frac{\partial V}{\partial g} = \frac{(T + (i - g)T')b^\theta K^\theta - (a + m(f + i))K}{(i - g)^2} \qquad [6.4]^{10}$$

Setting [6.3] and [6.4] equal to zero yields from [6.3]

$$K = \left(\frac{Tb^\theta \theta}{a + m(f + g)}\right)^n \qquad [6.5]$$

Where $T = 0$, $g = g_1$ which is the same result as setting $T = 0$ and $K = 0$ in [6.2] and falls steadily until on the horizontal axis

$$K_0 = \left(\frac{T(0)b^\theta \theta}{a + mf}\right)^n \qquad [6.6]$$

It clearly follows from [6.6] and [6.2] that $K_0 < K_v$ because $0 < \theta < 1$.

From [6.4] $\dfrac{\partial V}{\partial g} = 0$ when $K = 0$ and when

$$K = \left[\frac{(T + (i - g)T')b^\theta}{a + m(f + i)}\right]^n \qquad [6.7]$$

This curve Og_2K_g leaves the vertical axis at g_2 where g_2 is the root of $T + (i - g)T' = 0$. Now recalling that $T(g_1) = 0$ (see [6.5] and subsequent text) it follows that

$$T(g_1) + (i - g_1)T'(g_1) = (1 - g_1)T'(g_1) < 0.^{11}$$

In addition as

$$\frac{d}{dg}\left[T + (i - g)T'\right] = (i - g)T'' < 0$$

it follows that $g_2 < g_1$ as shown in Fig. 6.1. The curve cuts the horizontal axis at

$$K_g = \left[\frac{(T(0) + iT'(0))b^\theta}{a + m(f + i)}\right]^n \qquad [6.8]$$

While other cases are possible, only the case where $K_g > K_0$ is considered (it is drawn in Fig. 6.1). Considering only this possibility, it is clear that V is maximized at V^* where the loci of $\dfrac{\partial V}{\partial g} = 0$ and $\dfrac{\partial V}{\partial K} = 0$ cut at $(g^*,$ $K^*)$. Thus a firm can achieve maximum value V^* if it starts with capital goods of K^* and grows for ever at g^*. Faster growth produces lower value because the costs of faster expansion cancel larger sales. Similarly, if it had a larger capital it is worth less because its higher sales drive the price down too much. (The reader should draw a horizontal line for some $g > g^*$ and a vertical line for some $K > K^*$ to show for himself that the firm gets on to a lower contour.)

The above model as developed by Solow can be used to demonstrate the behaviour of owner-motivated and manager- (or, more accurately, growth-) motivated firms. It turns out that this model is particularly useful not only in demonstrating the nature of Marris and Williamson's models but also in showing the effects of certain changes in various parameters, such as taxes.

In both the owner-motivated and the manager-motivated firm the choice of both the initial stock of capital and the steady-state growth rate present a problem. Reference to the familiar idea of present value maximization presents the problem that it is not clear that a choice which produces a higher V is necessarily the right thing. Take the case where there is a choice between investing in two firms of equal growth rates, one of which has a higher V but also requires a larger stock of capital, i.e., larger K.

There are two approaches which Solow suggests for solving this problem. The simplest of these is to assume that the firm starts with a given vertical (it might have taken over a firm of this size). It then sets this vertical equal to the locus of $\dfrac{\partial V}{\partial g} = 0$.

The vertical is obviously just tangent to the highest contour. The alternative is more complicated but represents an important contribution to the theory of the firm, as it results in certain insights into shareholder, manager, and entrepreneurial behaviour. The shareholder presumably is interested in maximizing the value of his portfolio[12]. The manager is interested in growth (more of this in a moment). Thus the shareholder is concerned with finding a value of $\dfrac{\partial V}{\partial K} = j$, which can be solved to yield

$$K = \left[\frac{T(O)b^\theta \theta}{a + mf + ji - (j - m)g} \right]^n \qquad [6.9]$$

The curve corresponding to [6.9] can be plotted in Fig. 6.1. Notice then when $K = 0$, $T(g) = 0$ which implies $g = g_1$. It reaches the horizontal axis where

$$K = K_j = \left[\frac{T(O)b^\theta \theta}{a + mf + ji} \right]^n < K_1 \qquad [6.10]^{[13]}$$

Thus optimality for the owner-motivated firm is achieved at point ℓ where $g_1 K_j \left(\text{locus of } \dfrac{\partial V}{\partial K} = j \right)$ intersects $g_2 K_g \left(\text{locus of } \dfrac{\partial V}{\partial g} = 0 \right)$. This is an extension and correction of Marris's approach to maximizing the "valuation ratio", $\dfrac{V}{mK}$, which implies that the firm attains a certain average value per money unit of capital while Solow requires that it achieve a certain marginal value per money unit of capital[14]. Notice that point ℓ is clearly less than V^*. This emphasizes the earlier point that the shareholder is not interested in maximizing the market value of any particular firm.

Solow's model, in addition to being an extension of the neoclassical theory to encompass growth, is also important for its ability to summarize, extend, and perhaps correct the managerial theories of Marris and Williamson with their emphasis on growth. Theories of the firm which make growth an independent objective recognize that fast growth might be at the expense of profits. Indeed profits might be so low relative to assets as to make takeover an attractive prospect. The exact form that this constraint takes presents some problems as Solow is able to show in the case of both Marris' and Williamson's constraints. Both formulations present ambiguities regarding the initial scale of the firm. For example, Marris hypothesises that the firm seeks the largest growth rate consistent with a minimum valuation ratio (V/mK). From V in [6.1] it can be seen that the firm can meet any constraint on the valuation ratio and grow at very near g_1 by choosing a sufficiently small initial capital stock! Williamson argues that when the value of the firm falls below a certain proportion of the value achieved by a "profit maximizing" (as he calls it) firm then it is at risk of takeover. Again there is no reason why the firm should not choose a very small initial stock of capital consistent with a high growth rate.

Solow chooses a very simple way of overcoming the problem of the indeterminacy of initial scale. He simply assumes that initial scale is given by some historical accident. Then management simply chooses its steady-state growth rate. On this basis, comparison between growth (managerial) models and conventional (shareholder) type models can be made. This will now be done for two firms, Fisher Ltd and Marris Ltd[15].

With Solow's assumption that some level of capital stock $K < K^*$ is given, Fisher Ltd chooses the rate of growth maximizing its market value; it solves $\dfrac{\partial V}{\partial g} = 0$ for g_F. Marris Ltd chooses a larger rate of growth g_m constrained by the lower limit of the valuation ratio; it solves $V(g_m, K) = \bar{v}mK$ where $\bar{v}$ is equal to, or just under, one.

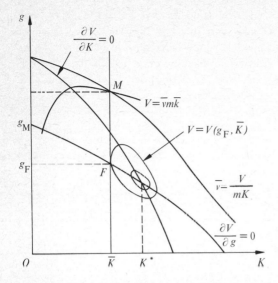

Thus in Fig. 6.2 $K = \bar{K}$ in the initial capital stock. Already $\dfrac{\partial V}{\partial g}$ has been worked out in [6.4], and the locus of $\dfrac{\partial V}{\partial g} = 0$

$$A = b^{-\theta} K^{1/n} = \frac{T(g) + (i - g)T'(g)}{a + m(f + i)} \qquad [6.11]$$

A is equal to the ratio of initial capital stock to initial gross sales revenue[16]. Thus for a given value of K, [6.11] is solved to yield point F as shown in Fig. 6.2.

To obtain the growth rate for Marris Ltd it is necessary to find where the vertical line corresponding to the initial stock of capital $\bar{K}$ cuts the curve along which $V = \bar{v}m\,\bar{K}$. This curve is given by[17]

$$A = \frac{T(g)}{a + m(f + \bar{v}i + (1 - \bar{v})g)} \qquad [6.12]$$

The curve corresponding to [6.12] is shown in the Fig. 6.2. It is clear that it implies a higher growth rate g_M and a lower market value. This can be seen by examining the point M where $\bar{K}$ cuts it in relation to point F. It also lies to the right of $\dfrac{\partial V}{\partial g} = 0$ (which follows from the fact that $T'(g) < 0$).

Solow's approach to treating the initial K as given means that the initial output and price are also given (because $Q = bK$, and $p = Q^{-1/n}$). Thus both types of firm would have the same price. In addition, Solow has formulated the effects of selling expenditures so that they shift the curve iso-elastically, otherwise this would imply different prices for the two types of firm. With these restrictions in mind it is possible to show the reactions of the two types of firm (as exemplified by Fisher Ltd and Marris Ltd) to various changes in environment.

The effect of a change in the price of capital goods (m) on the growth rate can easily be seen by references to [6.11] and [6.12] from which $\dfrac{dg_F}{dm}$ and $\dfrac{dg_M}{dm}$ can be derived after some manipulation.

$$\frac{dg_F}{dm} = \frac{(f + i)A}{(i - g_F)T''(g_F)} \tag{6.13}$$

$$\frac{dg_M}{dm} = \frac{(f + \bar{v}i + (1 - \bar{v})g_M)A}{T'(g_M) - (1 - \bar{v})mA} \tag{6.14}$$

Thus it is clear from [6.13] and [6.14] that the growth rate and the rate of investment decreases as m increases for both types of firm[18].

It is possible to say more by making the specific assumptions that

$$T(g) = 1 - S(g - g_m)^2,$$

where g_m is the growth rate that occurs when zero selling costs are incurred, and that $\bar{v} = 1$. Both firms, of course, choose a higher growth rate than g_m. With these assumptions

$$\frac{dg_F/dm}{dg_M/dm} = \frac{T'(g_M)}{(i - g_F)T''(g_F)} = \frac{g_M - g_m}{i - g_F} < 1 \tag{6.15}$$

It follows [6.15] is obviously less than one because even if g_F were nearly the same as g_F $i > g_M$. Thus Marris Ltd's investment is more sensitive to changes in the price than that of Fisher Ltd.

Solow is similarly able to show the effects of a change in the discount rate, the effect of an excise tax and the effect of a profits tax. The effect of an increase in the discount rate is to cause a fall in investment for both firms. Again, where a special form of $T(g)$ is chosen, it follows that Marris Ltd is more sensitive to changes in the discount rate than Fisher Ltd. For $\bar{v} = 1$, with an excise tax, z, the ratio of the two firms' responses

$$\frac{dg_F/dz}{dg_M/dz}$$

turns out to be the same as [6.14]. Thus both firms operate in qualitatively the same way, changes in excise taxes with Marris Ltd being possibly more sensitive. Again, a similar result applies to the effect of a proportional tax on profit; growth rates of both firms are reduced by an increase in this profit tax. The ratio given by [6.14] still applies.

Solow's model of steady-state growth of the firm is very important because it shows how qualitatively growth oriented and "profit" oriented firms respond in the same way to changes in environment. Thus an economist observing them would find it hard to distinguish one from the other. The fact that one chooses a higher growth rate might be important depending on the difference involved. These are all important results, depending on the nature of the selling cost function and perhaps the steady-state model. Further research in the area might well be directed to sensitivity analysis of assumptions about selling costs and steady state.

6.3 Risk, uncertainty, and the firm[19]

Like growth theory of the firm, the theory of the firm under uncertainty is not highly developed. Much of it is speculative. Thus what follows does not represent a comprehensive survey of uncertainty models, but rather the author's own views as to what represents potentially fruitful approach to the theory of the firm under uncertainty. Firstly, reference will be made to Cyert and March's behavioural theory and the firm and the role of uncertainty in it. This will lead to some further observations on the firm and its behaviour under uncertainty by Galbraith (1967) and Lintner (1970). Despite the rather provisional and undeveloped nature of the theory of the firm under uncertainty it is apparent that Lintner's model does raise some fundamental considerations on the relative significance of uncertainty and managerial motivation for the theory of the firm.

Cyert and March argued that firms recognized that uncertainty was one of the facts with which they had to live, and that their behaviour was strongly influenced by its presence. In particular, they argued that firms adopt various devices with the aim of avoiding uncertainty. For example, their decision procedures are such that each problem is solved as it occurs and the organization then waits for another problem to appear. In addition, rather than treating their environment as exogenous they seek ways of controlling it. Industry-wide organizations are notorious for such purposes. Things like "good business practice" are often standardized. As implied by the mark-up model of Chapter 5, rises in price would tend to be based upon common practice in the industry. The effect of this is clearly to reduce uncertainty considerably.

The extent to which firms are able to control their environment by such devices depends to a considerable extent on the market power or latent market power which they possess. This point was noticed and popularized by Galbraith (1967), whose controversial ideas attracted much criticism for the views it expressed on the extent to which large corporations control their economic and political environment. This matter is still subject to debate and still of considerable interest. However, of more importance here is his (testable) hypothesis that large corporations are prepared to forego a certain amount of profits to avoid uncertainty.

Lintner's model of decision making under uncertainty is particularly relevant to market situations where firms have substantial market power. It assumes in particular:

1.   Firms are price makers.

2.   At the time prices are determined the quantities of output which can be sold at any one of the possible prices during the period are uncertain.

3.   Marginal production costs are essentially constant with respect to output.

4.   While these types of firms are normally able to increase their expected quantities of output by increased advertising and promotion, it is assumed that such budgets are exogeneously fixed.

5.   Questions of optimal carry-over stocks have relatively little bearing on the price quoted by the firm at the beginning of the period.

6.   The uncertainty regarding the level of average variable costs is small compared with the uncertainty regarding price.

7.   Dynamic or interperiod interactions are ignored.

8.   Pricing decision are made on a fully rational profit maximizing basis subject to risk aversion with respect to the uncertain profits involved.

With these assumptions Lintner is able to construct a model of the firm which focuses on price-output decisions comparable with the neoclassical firm. The model also has the important feature that the degree of risk aversion can be explicitly incorporated into the analysis.

Lintner assumes that decisions are made on a profit-maximizing basis subject to risk aversion with respect to the uncertainties involved. This is a special case of assuming in a one period context that decisions are made to maximize end of period wealth $\tilde{W}_1$. (The tildes denote random variables throughout.) He also assumes the traditional Ramsey-de-Finetti-Savage axioms in constructing the firm's preference function which is risk averse. This requires $U'(W_1) > 0$ and $U''(W_1) < 0$. The actual degree of risk aversion is given by

$$r(W_1) = \frac{-U''}{U'} \qquad \text{(See Arrow, 1965; Pratt, 1964.)} \qquad [6.16]$$

The actual utility function is given by

$$U(\widetilde{W}_1) = a - b\,e^{-2\alpha \widetilde{W}_1} \tag{6.17}$$

where a, b, and α are all constants, and the degree of risk aversion from [6.16] is 2α.

If it is assumed that the distribution of the decisions taken by the firm is approximately normal (Gaussian) — $f(\widetilde{W}) = N\,[W^*,\ \sigma_w^2]$ where W^* is mean and σ_w^2 variance — then it follows that

$$E[U(\widetilde{W})] = a - b\,e^{-2\alpha(W^* - \alpha \sigma_w^2)} \tag{6.18}$$

As expected utility varies with the contents of the last bracket it follows that the decisions which maximize certainty equivalent $W = W^* - \alpha\sigma_W^2$ will also maximize expected utility.

Uncertain end-of-period wealth may be defined as

$$\widetilde{W}_1 = W_0 + \widetilde{\Pi}_1 \tag{6.19}$$

Thus $\bar{W}_1$ is taken to be a constant W_0 plus expected profit $\widetilde{\Pi}_1$. If it is further assumed that $\sigma_W^2 = \sigma_\pi^2$ it follows that the firm can be regarded as making price-output decisions such that

$$\hat{\Pi} = \Pi^* - \alpha\sigma_\pi^2 \tag{6.20}$$

is maximized. α is of course half the risk aversion inefficient and $\hat{\pi}$ is the certainty equivalent of profits.

It can readily be demonstrated how this works for the case where there is uncertainty about demand. This uncertainty is assumed to be independent of price charged; it is confined only to quantities sold. Thus the demand function under uncertainty is given by

$$\tilde{q} = f(p,\ \tilde{u}) = g(p) + \tilde{u} \tag{6.21}$$

where $g'(p) < 0$ and $\tilde{u}$ is a random term.

The above assumption regarding normally distributed random variable is retained throughout. Thus total revenue is given by

$$\widetilde{R}(p,\ \tilde{u}) = p\tilde{q} = pf(p,\ \tilde{u}) \tag{6.22}$$

With the assumption that marginal costs are constant over the relevant range total cost is given by

$$C(\tilde{q}) = F + v\tilde{q} \tag{6.23}$$

Thus the profit function is obtained from [6.22] and [6.23]

$$\widetilde{\Pi}(p,\ \tilde{u}) = p\tilde{q} - F - v\tilde{q} \tag{6.24}$$

where $\widetilde{\Pi}$ is a function of price (the decision variable) and $\tilde{u}$.

Expected profits are

$$\Pi^*(p) = pq^* - F - vq^* = (p - v)q^* - F \qquad [6.25]$$

where q^* is mean quantity demanded.

Variance of profit is

$$\sigma_\pi^2 = (p - v)^2 \sigma_u^2 \qquad [6.26]$$

Substitution of [6.25] and [6.26] in [6.20] yields

$$\hat{\Pi} = \Pi^* - \alpha\sigma_\pi^2 = (p - v)q^* - F - \alpha(p - v)^2 \sigma_u^2 \qquad [6.27]$$

The partial derivative of [6.27] with respect to $(-p)$ is

$$\frac{\partial\hat{\Pi}}{\partial(-p)} = \frac{\partial\Pi^*}{\partial(-p)} - \alpha\frac{\partial\sigma_\pi^2}{\partial(-p)} \qquad [6.28]$$

Thus the firm may be regarded as thinking of setting a high price and progressively reducing its price until the benefits of price reduction outweigh the costs, that is, [6.28] is equal to zero. If [6.28] is set equal to zero and solved for α the relationship between risk aversion and price can be noted.

$$\alpha = \frac{\partial\Pi^*/\partial(-p)}{\partial\sigma_\pi^2/\partial(-p)} \qquad [6.29]$$

Thus for a given price change the higher the degree of risk aversion the greater the increase in expected profits required by a firm in order to induce it to accept greater profit variability. The relationships between mean and variance is shown in Fig. 6.3 for two firms, firm 1 and firm 2.

Fig. 6.3

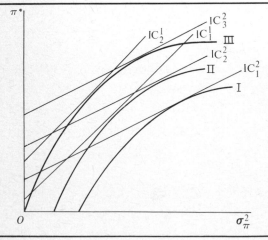

Indifference curves, whose slope is the value of [6.29], showing the firm's preference between mean profit and variance of profit are shown in Fig. 6.3. For firm 2 the slope is less steep than firm 1 implying that firm 2 is less risk averse than firm 1. The firm attains optimality when its indifference curve is tangential to the opportunity set (I, II, III) which show the actual feasible combinations of mean and variance of profit available to the firms. It is quite clear that firm 1 always prefers lower mean and lower variance to firm 2. It will thus trade profits for less risk.

It remains to show the effects of risk aversion on price and output and then compare the behaviour of the firm with other (certainty) models of the firm. Perhaps the simplest way of illustrating the significance and interpretation [6.28] is to do as Lintner does and take the case of a linear demand function with additive error term. Thus [6.21] takes the special form of

$$\tilde{q} = a - bp + \tilde{u}, \tag{6.30}$$

where a and b are both positive, expected quantity demanded from [6.30] becomes

$$q^* = a - bp \tag{6.31}$$

If [6.31] is substituted into [6.27] the derivative with respect to $(-p)$ becomes

$$\frac{\partial \hat{\Pi}}{\partial(-p)} = 2bp - a - bv + 2\alpha(p - v)\sigma_u^2 = 0 \tag{6.32}$$

[6.32] is solved for optimal price p to yield

$$p = \frac{a + bv + 2\alpha v\, \sigma_u^2}{2(b + \alpha\, \sigma_u^2)} = v + \frac{a - bv}{2(b + \alpha\, \sigma_u^2)} \tag{6.33}$$

To obtain, from these results, the case of profit maximizing under certainty it is necessary to set σ_u^2 (and therefore σ_π^2) equal to zero. Thus it is clear from [6.33] that any increase in α or σ_u^2 will reduce the value of $a - bv$ and hence reduce price. Thus prices will be lower (a) the greater the uncertainty and (b) the greater the risk aversion the closer price gets to marginal cost and therefore the farther away the firm with monopoly power gets from the monopoly (MR = MC) solution[20].

There are other important results that can be derived from the model. For example, the greater the uncertainty regarding sales and volumes and the greater the risk aversion of management the greater will be the expected quantity sold. This follows from the assumption of downward-sloping demand and as a corollary to the proposition that risk aversion and uncertainty reduces prices *ceteris paribus*. Thus uncertainty and risk aversion tend to reduce the traditional distortions attributed to the presence of monopoly distortions. The effects of corporate income taxes can also be derived[21].

The main effect of increasing corporate income taxes is to have the same effects as reducing risk aversion. This implies that increasing these taxes will cause (*ceteris paribus*) an increase in prices, and profit margins. Increasing these taxes will increase the severity of the traditional monopoly distortions ascribed to monopolistic markets.

The comparison between these results and the sales maximizing and managerial utility models of Baumol and Williamson is striking. It would appear to raise the need for empirical investigation into the possibility that uncertainty and risk aversion might account for many of the phenomena attributed to other goals in the managerial literature.

6.4 Conclusion

The topics surveyed in this chapter are perhaps the most important areas of development of the theory of the firm at the moment. The actual models chosen are probably amongst the simplest, and richest, available at the moment. There are other possibilities, as mentioned concurrently with the development of the models. The scope for future research is considerable. In particular, the idea of a synthesis of a stochastic growth model of the firm would appear to combine some of the major features of sections 2 and 3. This might involve sensitivity analysis to determine to what extent alternative motivation to profit maximization leads to different results. Indeed there is considerable scope for the study of motivation and uncertainty as Heal and Silberston (1972) have noted. Their approach was to note that managers and shareholders might have different assessments of the uncertainties facing the firm and show the implications on growth of the firm. Thus if shareholders, being less well informed, attach greater importance to the uncertainty facing the firm Heal and Silberston argue that this would cause them to adopt a shorter time horizon or higher discount rate than the managers. In terms of their model this would imply a reduction in the growth rate and move the firm closer to the conventionally motivated firm (which in the growth maximizing context is assumed to maximize present value).

All this serves to underline the point implied at the start of section 6.3, that the introduction of uncertainty into the theory of the firm means that the generality of the neoclassical theory is no longer attainable. This is illustrated by Day, Aigner and Smith (1971) who present essentially an alternative approach to that adopted by Lintner of maximizing an explicit utility function. Their approach is concerned with the idea of minimizing the probability of disaster which, by utilizing the Tchebycheff inequality, avoids the prior knowledge implied in maximizing an explicit utility function[22]. Instead it rests upon the nature and level of disaster whose probability is being minimized. Indeed price, output, mean and variance of profit depend upon these.

A further reason why generality is not obtainable under uncertainty arises from the fact that uncertainty may take so many forms. It may, for instance, take the form of uncertainty about quantity sold as in the Lintner (1970) example, or take the form of uncertainty about realized prices. Day, Aigner and Smith (1971) allow realized prices to be subject to random variations. The effect of this is to imply that price is set higher than the monopoly (MR = MC) solution, the greater the degree of risk aversion in contrast to the results of Lintner (1970) model[23]. This difference in the nature of uncertainty causes these qualitatively opposite effects, as noted by Lintner himself[24].

Thus the observations by Heal and Silberston in the context of a dynamic model stand out in contrast to Lintner's results for a static model. This, and Day, Aigner and Smith's results, imply a lack of generality in the current theory of the firm under uncertainty. It seems likely that any attempt at generality is pointless, that future research will lead along the lines of refining uncertainty models, extending their scope, and reconciling conflicting results produced by them. In any event there would appear to be scope for considerable future research in this area.

Exercises — 6

1. If a corporate income tax of t is imposed the firm's profit function [6.27] becomes

$$\hat{\Pi}_t = (1 - t)\Pi^* - \alpha(1 - t)^2 \sigma_\pi^2$$

From this derive the effects on price and output, etc., mentioned in the text.

2. Show that both firms reduce the growth rate as a result of a rise in the discount rate. Show that Marris Ltd is more sensitive to changes in the discount rate than Fisher Ltd where $T(g)$ has the special quadratic form, $1 - S(g - g_m)^2$.

146

Notes

1.   This is by no means a view universally held by economists. Several excellent books on the theory of the firm have little or no discussion of the general equilibrium approach, e.g., Horowitz (1970), Naylor and Vernon (1969).

2.   Perhaps the most significant authoritative treatment of general equilibrium is Arrow and Hahn (1972). Other books include Keunne (1963) and Triffin (1942). Articles include Negishi (1960), Archibald (1971) and for an example of the pitfalls involved with the monopolist in general equilibrium see Davis and Whinston (1965, 1967) and Negishi (1967).

3.   Take, for example, the implications of the equilibrium wage for all the cross-connections involved. Equilibrium then for workers results in a wage at which consumers, in exercising their work/leisure choice, supply all the labour actually used, at which the resulting income is just enough to enable them to buy just the goods produced at equilibrium prices, at which firms, given equilibrium outputs and prices, will choose to employ the labour actually supplied, and at which, given all the alternative production processes, the producers will combine quantities of other inputs with the equilibrium amount of labour.

4.   Because in an exchange economy

$$\sum_{i=1}^{n} p_i X_i^s = \sum_{i=1}^{n} p_i X_i^d,$$

where the p's are the exchange ratios, the X_i^s, and X_i^d the quantities supplied and demanded respectively, it follows that if $n-1$ markets are in equilibrium the n'th is in equilibrium. Thus only $n-1$ equations are needed. For details in the form of a simple introductory discussion of Walras' law, see Tisdell (1973) or Henderson and Quandt (1971, pp. 159–71).

5.   This is really a rather weak qualification. It excludes cases where some consumers have absolutely nothing of value and receive no transfer of income.

6.   Arrow's analysis is repeated with certain points of clarification in Arrow and Hahn (1972, pp. 151–68).

7.   In economics it is quite usual to make steady-state type assumptions because they enable a dynamic problem to be analysed by means of static

model. The alternative to steady state assumptions is a more complicated approach employing variational methods, which have been employed in macroeconomic growth models for some considerable time, e.g., Ramsey (1927).

8. $S(g)$ is assumed convex and $S(g_m) = 0$ where g_m is growth with no selling expenditure.

9. This is derived as follows

From [6.1], $0 = \dfrac{T(g)b^\theta K^\theta - (a + m(f + g))K}{i - g}$

Dividing both sides by $i - g$ and taking $(a + m(f+g))K$ to the left-hand side.

$(a + m(f + g))K = T(g)b^\theta K^\theta$

Dividing the left-hand side by K and the right-hand side by $a + m(f + g)$ yields

$K^{1-\theta} = \dfrac{T(g)b^\theta}{a + m(f + g)}$

As $1 - \theta = \dfrac{1}{n}$

$K = \left(\dfrac{T(g)b^\theta}{a + m(f + g)}\right)^n$

10. [6.4] is derived as follows:

Differentiate with respect to g using quotient rule

$$\frac{\partial V}{\partial g} = \frac{(i - g)(T'b^\theta K^\theta - mK) + [Tb^\theta K^\theta - (a + m(f + g))K]}{(i - g)^2}$$

$$= \frac{[T + (i - g)T']b^\theta K^\theta - [a + m(f + g) + (i - g)m]K}{(i - g)^2}$$

where $T = T(g)$ and $T' = T'(g)$.

11. Recall $T(g) = 1 - S(g)$ and $S(g)$ is a non-decreasing convex function making $T'(g) < 0$ whenever $g \geqslant 0$.

12. It might be expected that the entrepreneur would also have this objective. However, this raises a potentially important problem. In

practice, an entrepreneur has bounded rationality; actually being an entrepreneur (or perhaps more accurately, owner-manager) might take up every bit of his ability. His problem is that he cannot find time to get the information required to maximize the value of his portfolio in the same way as the shareholder is assumed to do this. Thus he may not actually invest in alternative firms which would provide him with more wealth at the margin.

13. The curve either falls all along or bends back once only. Solow shows this by providing

$$\frac{dK}{dg} < 0 \quad \text{and} \quad \frac{d^2K}{dg^2} < 0.$$

14. For a definition of the valuation ratio see Marris (1964, pp. 21–2). For a statement of Marris's models see Marris (1964, pp. 224–65), and Marris and Wood (1971, pp. 17–36).

15. Actually Solow also considers a simple case of Williamson Inc. However, as the Williamson criterion is more complicated, and not inherently more plausible, it will not be examined here. Solow's titles for the two types of firm, Fisher Inc and Marris Inc, have been retained.

16. This is derived from [6.4] as follows

Writing [6.4] as $0 = (T + (i - g)T') b^\theta K^\theta - (a + m(f + i))K$ which can be written as $(a + m(f + i))K = (T + (i - g)T')b^\theta K^\theta$ which yields

$$Kb^{-\theta}K^{-\theta} = \frac{(T + (i - g)T')}{a + m(f + i)}$$

As $KK^{-\theta} = K^{1-\theta} = K^{1-[1-(1/n)]} = K^{1/n}$ it is clear how [6.11] is derived.

To show that $b^{-\theta}K^{1/n}$ = ratio of initial capital stock to sales recall that sales $= Q^\theta = b^\theta K^\theta$ and initial capital stock $= K$ thus

$$\frac{K}{b^\theta K^\theta} = b^{-\theta}K^{1-\theta} = b^{-\theta}K^{1/n}.$$

17. This is derived by manipulating [6.1]. Putting $V = \bar{v}mK$ and multiplying by $(i - g)$ yields $(i - g)\bar{v}mK = Tb^\theta K^\theta - (a + m(f + g))K$. Taking the second term of the right-hand side across to the left-hand side yields $(i - g)\bar{v}mK - (a + m(f + g))K = Tb^\theta K^\theta$.

Dividing by K, exchanging numerator and denominator, etc., yields [6.12].

18. In view of the assumption that $S(g)$ is a convex function it follows that $T'(g) < 0$ and $T''(g) < 0$; since $i > g_M > g_F$ it follows that [6.13] and [6.14] are both of negative sign.

19. Sometimes the distinction is made between certainty, objective, risk, subjective risk, and uncertainty. Objective risk implies that an objective basis exists for computing the probabilities of various possible outcomes. Subjective risk refers to the case where an economic agent feels able to determine the probabilities. Uncertainty refers to the case where neither of these is possible. No further comment on these definitions will follow; suffice it to say that this section is concerned with situations other than certainty.

20. This point can be further emphasized by taking the total differential of [6.28] and then determining the effect of p of changes in σ_u^2.

(The total differential is

$$\frac{\partial^2 \hat{\Pi}}{\partial p^2} \, dp + \frac{\partial^2 \hat{\Pi}}{\partial p \partial \sigma_u^2} \, d\sigma_u^2 = 0$$

and the effect of σ_u^2 on p is obtained from this as

$$\frac{dp}{d\sigma_u^2} = -\frac{\partial^2 \hat{\Pi}/\partial p \partial \sigma_u^2}{\partial^2 \hat{\Pi}/\partial p^2}.)$$

This last expression is negative because $\dfrac{\partial^2 \hat{\Pi}}{\partial p^2} < 0$ (for a maximum) and

$$\frac{\partial^2 \hat{\Pi}}{\partial p \partial \sigma^2} = -2\alpha(p - v) < 0 \text{ for all } p > v.$$

21. The reader is encouraged to do this himself as an exercise at the end of this chapter.

22. Principally they discuss the idea of safety margins as discussed much earlier by Fellner (1948) and their relationship with Roy's notion of safety first (Roy, 1952).

23. See Day, Aigner, and Smith (1971, p. 1294). In view of the fact that the development of Day, Aigner, and Smith appeared independently of Lintner, they do not relate their results to the model developed by Lintner. Similarly, the development of Leland (1972) is independent of Day, Aigner, and Smith (1971) and also of Lintner (1970).

24. He states, "It will be found that, if independent of the price quoted, the effect of uncertainties with respect to costs, realized prices and profit margins are qualitatively opposite to those found for quantity uncertainty — an important fact which seems to have been overlooked in the literature." (Lintner, 1970, p. 258.)

7

Theories of the firm and public policy

There has been a long tradition of public concern about the effects of firm and industry behaviour on the rest of the economy and society in general. More recently this interest has expressed itself in concern about the activities of multinational corporations and the effects of industry on the natural environment. The purpose of this chapter is to show how the theory of the firm is relevant in the analysis of problems of public policy concerning the firm and industry. Thus section 7.1 will be concerned with showing something on the forms which public policy toward the firm has taken and how the scope of public policy is extending. Section 7.2 will be concerned with some of the possible implications of recent developments in the theory of the firm and welfare economics for the analysis of public policy. Section 7.3 will be concerned with the implications of some empirical work on the firm for public policy. Finally, Section 7.4 will provide a discussion of some of the scope for future research.

7.1 The development of public policy toward the firm
With the development of industrialization there has been an increasing concern by government to protect individuals and society from certain features of the activities of firms. For example, the early legislation in the UK was concerned with regulating the conditions of work of child labour. Very recently there has been an increasing concern with the productive activities of firms in so far as they affect the natural environment. Both of these instances epitomize the nature of government interest in the firm. Government feels obliged to intervene in the activities of firms because the environment in which firms operate lacks the ability to control the firm. With the advances in technology and growing complexity of firms on the one hand, and the tendency for government to assume responsibility for

an increasing number of activities on the other hand, it is apparent that the firm has become subject to an increasing number of controls over the last hundred years or so, and will become subject to more control in the future. While it is beyond the scope of this book to discuss the development of government control over industry, it is now proposed briefly to state this thesis of increasing government involvement with firms and suggest some of its possible effects.

From an early stage public policy has been concerned with the issues involved where a firm (or firms) possessed market power[1]. The consolidation and growth of American industry after the Civil War and the abuses of market power with the creation of trusts led to the first important piece of legislation relating to market power in modern industry with the Sherman Act of 1890. This landmark in antitrust law was followed in 1914 by the Clayton Act which together with the Sherman Act laid the basis of US antitrust policy, and was the forerunner to the policies directed against market power in the UK after the Second World War. Antitrust laws aim to harmonize the profit-seeking behaviour of firms with the public interest. They do this by prohibiting certain kinds of conduct by firms and by shaping (or reshaping) market structure along competitive lines. The latter, as will be indicated in the next section, thus aims to produce a system which will produce conduct which is in the public interest.

The problem of market power of public utilities was also recognized in the early days. These are regarded as different from other types of business enterprise. For example, the public utilities in the US were exempted from the antitrust laws, instead they were subject to regulation by a regulatory commission. In the UK the tendency has been to bring public utilities under increasing control in the form of public ownership. The public utility is "different" from other firms in that it involves overwhelming economies of scale. In view of the fact that the utility has to provide a system for transmitting its product connecting an additional consumer to its system can be done at very low (relatively) marginal cost. Similarly, rivalry from another competitor through provision of another network in the same area results in costly duplication of facilities and many infuriating and expensive external effects like the need to dig up the streets more often[2]. Thus public utilities are usually referred to as "natural monopolies" because the minimum scale of production is such as to make it impossible for more than one firm to enjoy all the (considerable) economies of scale in a particular market. Recently there has been a tendency amongst economists to attempt to apply the developments in the theory of the firm to public utilities and to question the policies of regulations currently being employed. For example, Averch and Johnson (1962) employed the profit maximizing model of the firm subject to regulation and showed that the firm would, in its desire to maximize profits, choose a non-optimal factor combination for its chosen level of output. This arises from the fact that regulation took the form of fixing a maximum rate of return which the firm might attain. Averch and Johnson's paper was important in that it attracted attention at an early stage to the likelihood that regulation, in attempting to cure one sympton of monopoly, namely price in excess of marginal cost, created other problems. This was recognized also in the managerial theories of the firm. Williamson (1967), for example, indicated how regulated "managerial" firms would tend to hire more staff and pay more profit out in emoluments than non-regulated "managerial" firms. These kinds of tendencies have become increasingly important as will be indicated in the next section where some new developments on the welfare losses from market power are discussed.

Antitrust and regulation are the two traditional areas of government intervention in the operation of firms. However, government is continually extending the nature of its control over industry. For example, the traditional area of antitrust is having to be extended to consider the effects of conglomerate mergers[3]. Considerations of research and development are problems considered in the context of antitrust and merger policies. It is sometimes argued that research and development is only economical in large units and hence is a justification for mergers.

Government is becoming increasingly interested in the role of firms in technological advances. Its involvement often is direct, in that it places many contracts with firms the effect of which is some research spillovers whose relevance extends beyond the firm. Governments, in entering contracts with firms, run into several problems. Sometimes the risks involved are too much for the firms, and the government ends up by assuming them. Sometimes firms exist only because the government is prepared to place contracts. For example, the UK and US aerospace industries have become increasingly dependent on government business. In such cases any trace of market discipline disappears, and economists have become interested in devising forms of government contract which act as an alternative to the discipline provided by the market[4]. While such contracts form an important advance upon what has previously happened with the type of full-cost pricing contracts which were supposed to give a reasonable profit, it seems likely that advances in this area will need to go in line with advances in the theory of the firm. An example of this might be the design of an incentive contract on the basis of a rather simple view of profit maximization.

Government has become increasingly involved as a producer in its own right with the expansion of education, health, social, and local government services. Many of the problems encountered in these kinds of productive activities are encountered in firms producing for the market or for govern-ment. These kinds of productive organizations are clearly not profit moti-vated; however, like firms they are likely to be managerially motivated. It is not clear, lacking even the controls exerted by the product and capital markets, what alternatives government can impose upon its own creatures.

Government has, since the end of the Second World War, been con-cerned with maintaining a growing economy with so-called full employ-ment, stable prices, balanced international payments, and various other responsibilities for macro and regional aspects of the economy. This has led it to further controls of firms. For example, regional policy has led to a ban on expansion in some regions and incentives in the form of grants or tax concessions where market forces were failing to attract industry to a particular area. Recently governments, particularly in the US and UK, have attempted to impose general controls of prices and incomes. This has led to an increasing involvement of the executive with the almost day-to-day running of industry[5].

Finally, the increasing concern for preserving the natural environment and the concern of many economists with the failure of the market mechanism to conserve natural resources and to control pollution will further involve government in the control of industry. It is possible that many traditional concerns with growth, production, and industry will have to be radically modified and that government will have to take even more responsibility for firms and industry than has yet been envisaged. Some idea of the implications for the theory of the firm of this trend toward further government involvement will be discussed in section 7.4.

7.2 Some implications of recent developments

The increasing scope of public policy toward the firm and the advances in the theory of the firm have taken place concurrently with advances in welfare economics and ways of measuring the welfare loss from the exercise of market power by firms. The recent developments in the theory of the firm imply different behaviour from the neoclassical profit-maximizing firm. The result is that the traditional measure of the welfare loss from monopoly needs to be modified. A simple diagrammatic treat-ment follows, which follows from the contributions of Comanor and Leibenstein (1969)[6].

The traditional measure of welfare loss is the triangle (Marshallian triangle) formed by taking the excess of price above marginal cost. However, to take into account the effects of recent developments in the theory of the firm in measuring the welfare loss from monopoly it is assumed that costs are higher under monopoly than under competition.

Fig. 7.1

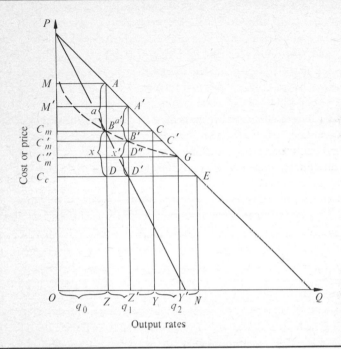

Output rates

Thus in terms of Fig. 7.1 monopoly costs are given by C_m and competitive costs by C_c. The apparent or perceived welfare loss from monopoly is defined as W_a. This is where the traditional Marshallian triangle approach falls down in the presence of X-inefficiency. It is only possible to perceive actual costs of C_m and therefore $W_a = ABC$. The full measure of this allocative inefficiency is actually given by W_{ax} which is the triangle by ADE, when the higher costs of the monopoly firm are taken into account. Additionally, there is the welfare loss from the X-inefficiency itself to be taken into account. This is given by W_x or the difference between competitive and monopolistic total costs which is clearly $C_m C_c DB$ in Fig. 7.1. It should be noticed that this loss has no allocative component. The changes in output are represented by q_1 and q_2. Thus q_1 is the difference in output between competition and monopoly exclusive of the cost effect, and q_2 is the difference directly associated with the cost reduction.

The difference between the traditional analysis of the welfare loss from monopoly and the above approach by Comanor and Leibenstein is apparent. However, before going on to discuss the implications of this approach for public policy it will prove useful to examine an extension to the Comanor and Leibenstein approach. Implicit in the above summary of the Comanor and Leibenstein case is the assumption that X-inefficiency affects only marginal cost. The alternative extreme, that X-inefficiency is an overhead effect and, therefore, affects only fixed costs, will now be examined. In such circumstances the monopoly output rate with X-inefficiency would be $OZ' > OZ$ where marginal cost is equated with marginal revenue. The monopoly price would be $A'Z' = OM' < OM$. In order to retain — for purposes of comparison — the same level of total costs as in the case described above it is necessary to construct through B a rectangular hyperbola which will cut the demand curve between C and E at G, in which case average cost, including overhead X-inefficiency, of producing the monopoly output is C'_m, given by the intersection of $A'Z'$ with the rectangular hyperbola $BB'G$.

The relevant welfare losses in this case are derived in similar manner to the above case. The welfare loss from monopoly-induced X-inefficiency is W'_x or $C'_m C_c D'B'$, which is equal to W_x by assumption and the construction of the rectangular hyperbola $BB'G$. The apparent partial welfare loss from allocative inefficiency is W'_a, or $A'B'C'$ (where $W'_a \gtreqless W_a$). The total measure of allocative inefficiency is W'_{ax}, which is the triangle $A'D'E$, which is less than ADE or W_{ax}. The total output adjustment in the overhead case $Z'N$ is clearly less than that in the Comanor and Leibenstein case described above, ZN. The q_2 component which features in Comanor and Leibenstein's case has no counterpart in the overhead effect in which case marginal cost is unaffected by X-inefficiency.

In addition to the two polar cases discussed above it is possible to derive four intermediate cases. These illustrate the relevance of the analysis for public policy in the field of antitrust and regulation.

Case 1a: Full competitive X-efficiency
It is evident that the usual first-best case for competition is enhanced by the introduction of the X-effect in that additional welfare gains are provided in the form of $W_{ax} = W_a + W_x$. Since W_{ax} is always greater than W_a, the overall X-effect must always strengthen the first-best case in favour of competition. Where second-best conditions exist, however, the deadweight loss attributable to monopoly no longer constitutes an unambiguous case in favour of competition, since the required reallocation of factor inputs may worsen total welfare. Even where the allocative effect was negative, the introduction of X-efficiency would provide a counteracting element and would thereby enhance the likelihood that a single-industry shift from monopoly to competition would improve economic welfare.

Case 1b: Full competitive X-efficiency: overhead effect
Once again, the usual first-best case for competition is enhanced by the introduction of the X-effect in that additional welfare gains are provided in the form of $W'_{ax} = W'_a + W'_x$. Since W'_{ax} is always greater than W'_a, the overall X-effect will always strengthen the first-best case in favour of competition. On the other hand, since $W'_{ax} < W_{ax}$ and $W'_x = W_x$, the overhead effect case offers less powerful additional support for competition under first-best conditions than does the Comanor–Leibenstein case. By contrast, under second-best conditions, such as those previously discussed, the case in favour of monopoly is comparatively better supported in the overhead effect case than in the Comanor–Leibenstein case.

Case 2a: "Competitive" X-inefficiency
This case represents an intermediate solution, in which a "competitive" price solution is achieved but X-inefficiency persists. It is highly probable that regulatory intervention of the public utility type (as a substitute for antitrust) might achieve some such result, especially where the regulatory commission was denied access to detailed cost data. The output rate attained under this solution would be OY at the price OC_m, and the associated first-best welfare gain would be W_a. Under second-best conditions this solution conceivably might worsen total welfare, by comparison with the straightforward monopoly solution.

Case 2b: "Competitive" X-inefficiency: overhead effect
On the assumption that regulatory intervention was successful in attaining an average-cost pricing solution but failed to eliminate X-inefficiency, the relevant output rate in Fig. 7.1 would be OY' and the corresponding price would be $Y'G = OC''_m$. The unambiguous first-best welfare improvement is represented by the triangle $A'D''G$. Under second-best conditions this solution conceivably might worsen total welfare by comparison with the straightforward monopoly solution.

Case 3a: Monopolistic X-efficiency
This case represents an intermediate solution, in which a monopolistic price solution is accepted but X-inefficiency is eliminated, perhaps by a regulatory commission motivated to achieve technological efficiency but undecided as to the policy significance of allocative "inefficiency". The relevant output rate would be OZ' (the same as the overhead effect case), and the price would be OM'. The welfare gain is unambiguous both under first-best and under second-best conditions.

Case 3b: Monopolistic X-efficiency: overhead effect
On the assumption that regulatory intervention succeeded in eliminating overhead X-inefficiency but retained monopoly conditions, there would be

no impact either upon the output rate, OZ', or upon price, OM'. The welfare gain is again unambiguous, both under first-best and under second-best conditions.

From the above analysis it is clear that the case for antitrust is usually strengthened. However, in emphasizing the perceived costs of the monopolist the above analysis has emphasized that argument implicit in the earlier analysis of the theory of the firm, that regulation of firms presents many more difficulties than was previously acknowledged[7].

As the above conclusion, and indeed the whole approach to X-inefficiency emphasized in this book, is not subject to universal agreement, it seems appropriate to state one of the recent and principal attacks on the approach set out in this chapter. This attack on the earlier conclusions and, indeed, the concept of X-inefficiency, was published shortly after the publication of the above papers by Comanor and Leibenstein and Crew and Rowley. The paper concerned, Parish and Ng (1972), explicitly attacked the Comanor and Leibenstein measure of welfare loss and implicitly attacked the very notion of X-inefficiency itself. Their arguments are interesting; thus a brief restatement and refutation of them will now follow.

Parish and Ng argue that the X-inefficiency effect — the increase in cost which arises from the monopolization of a competitive sector — is entirely absorbed as producers' surplus. They further argue that this producers' surplus is valued higher than the cost increase itself. Thus Parish and Ng's producers' surplus is treated as a benefit and not a cost as in the Comanor—Leibenstein measure. This means that the Parish—Ng measure of welfare loss turns out to be less even than W_{ax} (represented by triangle ADE), since the X-inefficiency is deducted from the welfare loss as measured by W_{ax}. But the Parish and Ng procedure is likely — in certain circumstances — to be misleading.

If Parish and Ng had simply drawn attention to the possibility that gains to workers might arise as a result of their getting some benefits from the extra resources used when X-inefficiency was present then they would have drawn attention to an important point not immediately obvious in the literature. However, to go far beyond this and argue that "presumably . . . the monopolist attached a greater value (or at least as great a value) to quiet living as these profits foregone" (Parish and Ng, 1972, p. 303) is possibly to misunderstand the concept of X-inefficiency and to substitute for it a concept of their own which is unlikely to be relevant to the kind of problems of market power met in modern industrialized economies. The relevance of their concept would seem to be confined to the old neoclassical entrepreneurial firm and seems likely to have almost no significance for the advances that have been made in the theory of the firm, at least in the last twenty years. They imply that the benefits from discretion arising from monopoly are entirely absorbed by the firm to provide greater benefits than the extra costs involved. However, on the basis of the theories discussed in earlier papers, there are several reasons why this is not likely to be so.

Firstly, there is the problem of division of spoils. Management and shop-floor always have found it very difficult to decide upon the relative share of the benefits going to each group within the firm. Typically they display a dog-in-the-manger attitude to each other, with the effect that the sum of benefits is not maximized. Indeed most industrial disputes are about division of spoils; it does not take an economist to see that many disputes result in both parties being worse off[8]. Hence it is unlikely that two conflicting groups could obtain benefits in excess of the costs arising from X-inefficiency.

Secondly, other institutional factors would militate against the producers' surplus being greater than the X-inefficiency increased costs. Because of mores regarding the use of capital as institutionalized in Company Law, many of the benefits desired by workers have to be taken surreptitiously making trade impossible. For example, an executive cannot trade his big carpeted office, his pretty secretary, his free telephone calls, his petrol for his wife's car, for say a cash payment. Moreover, these kinds of discretionary consumption are strictly restricted in their range. In addition, as he gets such items free, it is likely that he will "over-consume" such items to the extent that his marginal utility from them is less than their marginal cost. Similarly, a shop-floor employee may be forced to take reduced effort, or slacking on the job, when he would prefer to work harder for higher wages. He has just no opportunity to trade effort for wages in any optimal way. It thus seems unlikely that the extra costs of such consumption and reduced effort would exceed the benefits.

Thirdly, X-inefficiency is an insidious disease of non-competitive industry which creeps into the firm without anyone being aware of it. It builds up to large proportions with people "living off the fat" of the firm. A crisis occurs, say because of outside competition, and the firm having become flabby finds it hard to respond. Sometimes it responds successfully by cutting costs and its labour force. In a full employment economy the gains from such changes in the use of factors exceed the losses as the factors are all employed in alternative more profitable uses. O. E. Williamson has cited instances of this happening. It is thus very difficult to see how Parish and Ng can say that the benefits from X-inefficiency exceed the costs.

It therefore seems most unlikely that the Parish—Ng measure of welfare loss has much relevance to modern industrial economies with large corporations. Some reasons were given above why such organizations were unlikely to provide the mechanisms to enable the X-inefficiency to be taken as producers' surplus to the extent required by Parish and Ng. Their contribution, however, should not be ignored, although it is essentially one of degree. The whole of the additional costs involved as a result of X-inefficiency should not be treated as welfare loss. Some benefits do arise to workers from X-inefficiency. This, however, only necessitates a simple change to the analysis. In terms of the earlier analysis, all that is required is to state that "the welfare loss from X-inefficiency" = $W_x \leqslant C_m C_c DB$.

Thus Parish and Ng's arguments still leave the complex questions of the public policy and the firm open, and subject to further research and debate as to the nature of governmental intervention with the behaviour and environment faced by firms. It seems unlikely, however, that government should just let things be. There still seems to be a case for a structural approach which aims at a return to more competitive conditions.

7.3 Empirical research and public policy

Much of what has gone before has been theoretical. No attempt has been made to describe efforts to test the theories which have been presented. Clearly empirical questions do arise. For example, the nature of the public policy debate outlined in the present chapter depended upon the way actual firms behave. Certainly it is important to know if X-inefficiency is related to market power in the way implied by the earlier analysis.

Much empirical work remains to be done. A few examples, which in no sense represent a theory, will now be examined to give an idea of the nature of the empirical work that is being undertaken of direct relevance to the testing of the theories outlined in earlier chapters.

Williamson (1967) has produced various evidence in support of his theory of managerial discretion. He examined three "extreme instances" which considered case studies of firms that had suffered a severe setback. Usually this took the form of alarming fall in the demand for its products. The results of his case studies were generally consistent with his managerial models. For example, staff and emoluments were reduced following the setback. In addition, he performed a statistical analysis on a group of large firms in an attempt to see how firms responded to opportunities for discretion. He employed various indices of opportunities for discretion, for example, the extent of stockholder diffusion, and the extent of competition. He was concerned with noting the instances where firms did not respond to the opportunities for discretion, as clearly these would contradict his hypothesis. His regression revealed significant coefficients with signs as predicted by his theory in most instances[9].

Some empirical work relating sales-maximization to executive compensation has been performed by R. T. Masson (1971). His results implied that the executives of the large firms forming his sample were not generally motivated to be sales maximizers. In addition, he found that firms with executives ". . . whose financial interests are more closely parallel to the goals of the stockholders and the long-run profitability of the firm do indeed outperform other firms in stock return". (Masson, 1971, p. 1278—9.) Masson's results, despite the non-random nature of his sample, are also in line with some findings of Lewellen (1968, 1969) which suggest that the separation of ownership and control need not necessarily lead to managerial objectives widely divergent from present value maximization.

An attempt to test the hypothesis that firms with greater market power are more risk averse has been done with regard to banking in the US by F. R. Edwards and A. A. Heggestad (1973). Their results proved consistent with this view. However, they were not able to throw any light upon the reason for this result. In particular, they were not able to show that there is something about firms with market power which gives their managers a greater aversion to risk. This ability to distinguish might be important in linking the theory of the firm with organization theory which refers to the way modern organizations generate uncertainty.

This brief review of empirical research was intended to be in no sense comprehensive or detailed. It has merely referred to a few important contributions in the hope of giving the reader some of the flavour of the work being undertaken and helping him to see in context the theoretical developments described. A further aim was to imply that there was considerable scope for future research on the firm, as the empirical work on the "new" theories was still in its infancy.

7.4   Scope for future research in the theory of the firm and public policy
As indicated in the previous section, there is considerable scope for future research in empirical aspects of firm behaviour. There is also scope for considerable further work in the theory of the firm, and research into public policy and the firm. This chapter aims at discussing some areas for future research.

There exists considerable scope for further research linking organization theory with the theory of the firm. The scope for future research might involve a much more formal development of the decision making process within firms and how, internally, the firm adjusts to changes in its environment. This would put attempts by government to control of the firm on a more precise basis. It would also perhaps help clarify some of the problems of uncertainty and the firm which were discussed earlier. For example, if large organizations do generate uncertainty then the hypothesis that firms use their market power to reduce uncertainty may not be unreasonable. Indeed, as implied in Chapter 6, there exists considerable scope for future research into the theory of the firm under risk and uncertainty. Clearly the present state of theory in this area needs extending, not just on academic grounds, but additionally to provide the basis for policy that is becoming increasingly relevant in economics.

One feature of the modern firms, which has only briefly been discussed in the course of this book, is the implications for the theory of the firm and public policy of the emerging phenomenon of the firm which is able to influence and control its environment. Traditionally the firm in theory has been regarded as a reactor to its environment. Even the monopolist has had to take his demand and costs as given and then adjust his price to these. As indicated in Chapter 1 and later chapters certain firms can now decide how fast they will grow, and what features of their environment they wish to change. For example, a firm might alter its demand by advertising, or changing the nature of its product. A firm might transform its cost conditions in a relatively short period by investment in research and development and cost-saving innovation. Firms might control their environment because of their relationships with government. Arguably, these features can all be handled by familiar techniques, for example a different *ceteris paribus*. However, these matters are highly complex and require further consideration. They raise serious issues for public policy, since the firms' ability to control their environment extends to their ability to influence and reduce governmental's ability to control. This is true especially of multinational companies, which can have a great effect on government. Thus much of the research in this area will be in the field of the multinational firm.

As indicated earlier in this chapter, government has been aware for some considerable period of the desire by firms to control their environment through mergers. In view of the development of conglomerate mergers, as well as vertical mergers, there is scope for a more comprehensive theory of mergers. The growth theories of the firm discussed here did not deal with mergers, and such growth theories of the firm could explicitly consider mergers. This would widen the possibilities beyond just choosing initial capital and the growth rate. Similarly, considerations of the welfare implications of mergers along the lines of Williamson's tradeoff analysis could be examined[10]. Indeed the possibility should be considered that a merger might produce higher costs, more X-inefficiency, but still be undertaken by firms because of the advantages it offered the firm in controlling its environment. Again a theory of mergers might provide policy makers with a framework of analysis for such mergers[11].

A further development, in view of the apparent tendency for markets to decrease in relative importance, is for the emergence of new mechanisms of control and allocation. As indicated already, government provides directly the only employment for some firms, and in such situations the traditional disciplines of the market will need to be supplemented by further disciplines. Already work on such mechanisms is under consideration. For example, A. O. Hirschmann (1970) has argued that there exists other more important mechanisms other than the exit mechanism provided by the market[12]. The incorporation of such mechanisms into the theory of the firm is a possible area for future research.

Finally, economic theories of other productive agents, which operate either directly under government or on a non-profit basis, is up for development. It is possible that some of the current developments in the theory of the firm will provide a fruitful basis for development in this area[13].

Notes

1. Market power has been implicit in the earlier analysis. A definition is given by W. G. Shepherd as ". . . the ability of a market participant or group of participants (persons, firms, partnerships, or others) to influence price, quantity, and the nature of the product in the marketplace." (Shepherd, 1970, p. 11.)

2. Next time the reader sees a hole in the road he should note the telegraph, and electric cables, the gas mains, the water mains, the sewer system and imagine the further confusion that would result with duplication.

3. A conglomerate would usually operate on the basis of Williamson's M-form of organization. The individual companies in the conglomerate might be in completely different and non-competing products. Thus the traditional (and more recent) arguments about market power which are relevant in the cases of horizontal mergers are apparently not relevant here. Indeed, if Williamson's M-form hypothesis is relevant it could be argued that conglomerates, by increasing X-efficiency, had beneficial implications for the public interest.

4. The literature is developing in this field. For an interesting example see Cross (1970).

5.   For example, the National Board for Prices and Incomes (see Fels, 1972) and more recently the Price Commission in the UK have had to get involved in some aspects of the internal running of industry. Profit margin control, which is a feature of both recent US and UK policies, involves many aspects of firm organization which come into the provinces of the modern theory of the firm. For example, profit margins are related to the growth in output, which itself is a concern of growth theory of the firm.

6.   What follows is based upon the approach formulated in Crew and Rowley (1971), and draws directly from that paper.

7.   For a detailed argument, expressed rather strongly, see Crew and Rowley (1970 and 1971).

8.   They do recognize the scope for other possible outcomes because "... managers ... may be able to pursue quiet lives at no cost to themselves but at a cost to the owners." (Parish and Ng, 1972, p. 307.)

9.   For a detailed description see Williamson (1967, pp. 85—139).

10.   Williamson (1968) argues that there is a tradeoff between market power and cost savings that results from a merger.

11.   The literature is not entirely without theorizing on mergers. For example, see Singh (1971) and Newbould (1970). However, there is considerable scope for extension.

12.   The exit mechanism is the familiar punishment by the market for failure, viz. bankruptcy. Hirschman suggests a further significant device of "voice", which implies that in the absence of the market discipline the people involved complain and make their point some other way than by just not buying the commodity. Such a theoretical system, if further developed, might imply radically different approaches to monopolies for example.

13.   For an interesting approach to this kind of problem see Newhouse (1970) who presents a theory of non-profit institutions, giving a hospital as an example.

References

Alchian, A. A., "Uncertainty, Evolution and Economic Theory", *J. Political econ.*, **58** (1950): 211–21.

Alchian, A. A. and Demsetz, H., "Production, Information Costs and Economic Organization", *Am. econ. Rev.*, **62**, **5** (December 1972): 777–95.

Archibald, G. C., "Comments on Arrow". In Marris and Wood (1971): 111–17.

Arrow, K. J. (Ed.), *"Essays in the Theory of Risk Bearing"*, Yrjo Jahnssonin Saatio, Helsinki (1965).

Arrow, K. J., "The Firm in General Equilibrium". In Marris and Wood (1971): 68–110.

Arrow, K. J., "Existence of an Equilibrium for a Competitive Economy", *Econometrica*, **22** (1954): 265–90.

Arrow, K. J. and Hahn, F. H., *General Competitive Analysis*, Oliver & Boyd, Edinburgh (1972).

Arrow, K. J., Chenery, H. B., Minhas, B. and Solow, R., "Capital-Labour Substitution and Economic Efficiency", *Rev. econ. Statist.*, **43** (August 1961): 225–50.

Averch, H., and Johnson, L. L., "Behavior of the Firm Under Regulatory Constraint", *Am. econ. Rev.*, **52** (1962): 1052–69.

Baumol, W. J., *Business Behavior Value and Growth*, Harcourt, Brace & World, New York, Revised edition (1967).

Baumol, W. J., *Economic Theory and Operations Analysis*, Prentice-Hall, Englewood Cliffs (1972).

Baumol, W. J. and Quandt, R. E., "Rules of Thumb and Optimally Imperfect Decisions", *Am. econ. Rev.*, **54** (March 1964): 23—46.

Baumol, W. J. and Stewart, M., "On the Behavioural Theory of the Firm". In Marris and Wood (1971): 118—43.

Berle, A. A., and Means, G. C., *The Modern Corporation and Private Property*, Macmillan, New York (1932).

Brems, H., *Quantitative Economic Theory: a Synthetic Approach*, Wiley, New York (1968).

Caves, R. E., "Uncertainty, Market Structure and Performance: Galbraith as Conventional Wisdom". In Markham and Papanek (1970): 283—302.

Chamberlin, E. H., *Theory of Monopolistic Competition*, Harvard University Press, Cambridge (1933).

Chandler, A. D., *Strategy and Structure*, Doubleday, New York (1966).

Charnes, A. and Cooper, W. W., *Management Models and Industrial Applications of Linear Programming*, Wiley, New York (1961).

Coase, R. H., "The Nature of the Firm". In *Readings in Price Theory*, R. D. Irwin, Homewood (1952).

Coddington, A., *Theories of the Bargaining Process*, Allen & Unwin, London (1968).

Cournot, A. (Translated by N. T. Bacon), *Récherches sur les Principles Mathematique de la Théorie des Richesses*, Macmillan, New York (1897).

Comanor, W. S. and Leibenstein, H., "Allocative Efficiency, X-Efficiency and the Measurement of Welfare Losses", *Economica*, **36** (August 1969): 304—9.

Cowling, K. (ed.), *Market Structure and Corporate Behaviour*, Gray-Mills, London (1972).

Crew, M. A., Jones-Lee, M. W. and Rowley, C. K., "X-Theory versus Behavioral Theory", *Sth. econ. J.*, **38** (October 1971): 173—84.

Crew, M. A. and Kleindorfer, P. R., "Marshall and Turvey on Peak Load or Joint Product Pricing", *J. Political econ.*, **79**, 6 (November/December 1971): 1369—77.

Crew, M. A. and Rowley, C. K., "Anti-Trust Policy: Economics versus Management Science", *Moorgate and Wall Street* (Autumn 1970): 19—34.

Crew, M. A. and Rowley, C. K., "Anti-Trust Policy: The Application of Rules", *Moorgate and Wall Street* (Autumn 1971): 37—50.

Crew, M. A. and Rowley, C. K., "On Allocative Efficiency, X-Efficiency and the Measurement of Welfare Losses", *Economica*, **38** (May 1971): 199–203.

Cross, J. G., *The Economics of Bargaining*, Basic Books, New York (1969).

Cross, J. G., "Incentive Pricing and Utility Regulations", *Q. J. econ.*, **84** (May 1970): 236–53.

Cyert, R. M. and March, J. G., *A Behavioral Theory of the Firm*, Prentice-Hall, Englewood Cliffs (1963).

Davis, O. A. and Whinston, A. B., "Welfare Economics and the Theory of Second Best", *Rev. econ. Stud.*, **32** (January 1965): 1–14.

Davis, O. A. and Whinston, A. B., "Piecemeal Policy in the Theory of Second Best", *Rev. econ. Stud.*, **34** (July 1967): 323–31.

Day, R. H., "Profits, Learning and the Convergence of Satisficing to Marginalism", *Q. J. econ.*, **81** (May 1967): 302–11.

Day, R. H. and Tinney, E. H., "How to Cooperate in Business Without Really Trying: A Learning Model of Decentralized Decision Making", *J. Political econ.*, **76** (July 1968): 583–600.

Day, R. H., Review of "Behavioral Theory of the Firm", *Econometrica*, **32** (July 1964): 461–4.

Day, R. H., Aigner, D. and Smith, K. R., "Safety Margins and Profit Maximization in the Theory of the Firm", *J. Political econ.*, **79**, 6 (November/December 1971): 1293–1301.

Downs, A., *Economic Theory of Democracy*, Harper & Row, New York (1957).

Edgeworth, F. Y., *Mathematical Psychics*, R. K. Paul, London (1897).

Edwards, E. O., "The Analysis of Output Under Discrimination", *Econometrica*, **18** (April 1950): 163–72.

Edwards, F. R. and Heggestad, A. A., "Uncertainty, Market Structure, and Performance in Banking", *Q. J. econ.*, **87**, 3 (August 1973): 455–73.

Fellner, W., "Average Cost Pricing and the Theory of Uncertainty", *J. Political econ.*, **56** (June 1948): 249–52.

Fels, A., *The British Prices and Incomes Board*, Cambridge University Press, Cambridge (1972).

Ferguson, C. E., *Microeconomic Theory*, Irwin, New York (1969).

Gale, D., *Theory of Linear Economic Models*, McGraw-Hill, New York (1960).

Galbraith, J. K., *The New Industrial State*, Hamish Hamilton, London (1967).

Graaf, J. de V., *Theoretical Welfare Economics*, Cambridge University Press, Cambridge (1957).

Hadley, G., *Linear Programming*, Addison-Wesley, New York (1962).

Hadley, G., *Non-Linear and Dynamic Programming*, Addison-Wesley, New York (1964).

Hall, R. L. and Hitch, C. J., "Price Theory and Business Behaviour", Oxford econ. Pap., 2, May 1939: 12—45.

Heal, G. M. and Silberston, A., "Alternative Managerial Objectives: an Exploratory Note", *Oxford econ. Pap.*, 24 (July 1972): 137—50.

Heathfield, D. F., *Production Functions*, Macmillan Studies in Economics, London (1971).

Henderson, J. M. and Quandt, R. E., *Microeconomic Theory: a Mathematical Approach*, McGraw-Hill, New York, Second edition (1971).

Hicks, J. R., "Annual Survey of Economic Theory: The Theory of Monopoly", *Econometrica*, 3, 1 (February 1935).

Hirschman, A. O., *Exit, Voice and Loyalty*, Harvard University Press, Cambridge, Massachusetts (1970).

Horowitz, I., *Decision Making and the Theory of the Firm*, Holt, Rinehart & Winston, New York (1970).

Hotelling, H., "Stability in Competition", *Econ. J.*, 39 (March 1929): 41—57.

Kuenne, R. E., *Theory of General Economic Equilibrium*, Princeton University Press, Princeton (1963).

Lancaster, K., *Mathematical Economics*, Macmillan, New York (1968).

Leibenstein, H., "Allocative Efficiency versus X-Efficiency", *Am. econ. Rev.*, 56 (June 1966): 392—415.

Leibenstein, H., "Organizational or Frictional Equilibria, X-Efficiency, and the Rate of Innovation", *Q. J. econ.*, 83 (November 1969): 600—23.

Leibenstein, H., "Competition and X-Efficiency", *J. Political econ.*, 81 (June 1973).

Leland, H. E., "Theory of the Firm Facing Uncertain Demand", *Am. econ. Rev.,* **62** (June 1972): 278–92.

Lewellen, W. G., *Executive Compensation in Large Industrial Corporations,* National Bureau of Economic Research, New York (1968).

Lewellen, W. G., "Management and Ownership in the Large Firm", *J. Finance,* **24** (May 1969): 299–322.

Lintner, J., "The Impact of Uncertainty on the 'Traditional' Theory of the Firm". In Markham and Papanek (1970): 238–65.

Lloyd, C., *Microeconomic Analysis,* R. D. Irwin, New York (1967).

Lombardini, S., "Modern Monopolies in Economic Development". In Marris and Wood (1971): 242–69.

Machlup, F., "Marginal Analysis and Empirical Research", *Am. econ. Rev.,* **36** (September 1946): 768–83.

Machlup, F., "Theories of the Firm: Marginalist, Behavioral, Managerial", *Am. econ. Rev.,* **57** (March 1967): 1–33.

Markham, J. W. and Papanek, G. F., *Industrial Organization and Economic Development,* Houghton Miffin, New York (1970).

Marris, R. L., *Economic Theory of Managerial Capitalism,* Macmillan, London (1964).

Marris, R. L. and Wood, A. (eds.), *The Corporate Economy,* Macmillan, London (1971).

Marshall, A., *Principles of Economics,* Macmillan, London, Eighth edition (1920).

Masson, R. T., "Executive Motivations, Earnings, and Consequent Equity Performance", *J. Political econ.,* **79,** 6 (November 1971): 1278–92.

Mishan, E. J., "A Survey of Welfare Economics 1939–59", *Econ. J.,* **70** (June 1960): 197–256.

Modigliani, F. and Miller, M., "The Cost of Capital, Corporation Finance and the Theory of Investment", *Am. econ. Rev.,* **48** (June 1958): 261–97.

Modigliani, F. and Miller, M., "Dividend Policy, Growth and the Valuation of Shares", *J. Busin.,* **34** (October 1961): 411–33.

Nagel, E., "Assumptions in Economic Theory", *Am. econ. Rev.,* **53** (May 1963): 211–19.

Naylor, T. H. and Vernon, J. M., *Microeconomics and Decision Models of the Firm*, Harcourt, Brace & World, New York (1969).

Negishi, T., "Monopolistic Competition in General Equilibrium", *Rev. econ. Stud.*, **28** (June 1961): 196—201.

Negishi, T., "The Perceived Demand Curve in the Theory of Second Best", *Rev. econ. Stud.*, **34** (July 1967): 315—16.

Newbould, G. D., *Management and Merger Activity*, Guthstead, Liverpool (1970).

Newhouse, J. P., "The Economics of Non-Profit Organizations", *Am. econ. Rev.*, **60** (March 1970): 64—74.

Nordquist, G. L., "The Break-up of the Maximization Principle", *Q. Rev. econ. Busin.*, **5**, 3 (Fall 1965): 33—46.

Parish, R. and Ng, Y. K., "Monopoly, X-Efficiency and the Measurement of Welfare Losses", *Economica*, **39** (August 1972): 301—8.

Penrose, E. T., *The Theory of the Growth of the Firm*, Basil Blackwell, Oxford (1959).

Pratt, J., "Risk Aversion in the Small and the Large", *Econometrica*, **32** (January/April 1964): 122—36.

Ramsey, F. P., "A Mathematical Theory of Saving", *Econ. J.*, **37** (March 1927): 47—61.

Robinson, J., *Economics of Imperfect Competition*, Macmillan, London (1933).

Rosenberg, R., "Profit Constrained Revenue Maximization: a Note", *Am. econ. Rev.*, **61**, 1 (March 1971): 208—9.

Roy, A. D., "Safety First in the Holding of Assets", *Econometrica*, **20** (July 1952): 431—48.

Samuelson, P. A., *Foundations of Economic Analysis*, Harvard University Press, Cambridge (1947).

Scitovsky, T., "A Note on Profit Maximization and Its Implications", *Rev. econ. Stud.*, **11** (1943): 57—60.

Shepherd, W. G., *Market Power and Economic Welfare*, Random House, New York (1970).

Simon, H. A., *Administrative Behavior*, Macmillan, New York (1957).

Simon, H. A., "Theories of Decision Making in Economics and Behavioral Science", *Am. econ. Rev.*, **69** (1959): 253—80.

Simon, H. A., "On the Concept of Organizational Goal", *Admve. Sci. Q.*, **9** (June 1964): 1—22.

Singh, A., *Takeovers*, Cambridge University Press, Cambridge (1971).

Smith, A., "The Nature and Causes of the Wealth of Nations", *Encyclopaedia Britannica*, Chicago (1952).

Solow, R. M., "Some Implications of Alternative Criteria for the Firm". In Marris and Wood (1971): 318—42.

Sraffa, Piero, "The Laws of Returns Under Competitive Conditions", *Econ. J.*, **36**, 144 (December 1926): 335—50.

Thompson, V. A., *Modern Organization*, Alfred A. Knopf, New York (1961).

Tintner, G., "Theory of Choice Under Subject Risk and Uncertainty", *Econometrica*, **9** (October 1941a): 298—304.

Tintner, G., "The Pure Theory of Production Under Technological Risk and Uncertainty", *Econometrica*, **9** (October 1941b): 645—67.

Tintner, G., "The Theory of Production Under Non-Static Conditions", *J. Political econ.*, **50** (October 1942): 645—67.

Tisdell, C. A., *Microeconomics: The Theory of Economic Allocation*, Wiley, Sydney (1973).

Triffin, R., *Monopolistic Competition and General Equilibrium Theory*, Harvard University Press, Cambridge (1942).

Walras, L. (Translated by William Jaffé), *Elements of Pure Economics*, Allen & Unwin, London (1954).

Wenders, J. T., "Collusion and Entry", *J. Political econ.*, **79**, 6 (November/December 1971): 1258—77.

Williamson, J. H., "Profits, Growth and Sales Maximization", *Economica*, **33** (February 1966): 1—16.

Williamson, O. E., *Economics of Discretionary Behavior: Managerial Objectives in a Theory of the Firm*, Markham Publishing, Chicago (1967).

Williamson, O. E., "Economies as an Antitrust Defense: The Welfare Tradeoffs", *Am. econ. Rev.*, **58** (March 1968): 11—31.

Williamson, O. E., *Corporate Control and Business Behavior*, Prentice-Hall, Englewood Cliffs (1970).

Solutions and hints to selected problems

Chapter 2

1. (a) $(1 - \alpha)r_1 x_1 - \alpha r_2 x_2 = 0$

    (b) Recall that the expansion path can be derived by equating the MRTS with the input price ratio to give

    $$\frac{\alpha}{1 - \alpha}\left(\frac{x_2}{x_1}\right)^{1/\sigma} = \frac{r_1}{r_2} \quad \text{where} \quad \sigma = \frac{1}{1 + \rho}$$

    or $\dfrac{x_2}{x_1} = b\left(\dfrac{r_1}{r_2}\right)^{\sigma}, \quad \text{where} \quad b = \left(\dfrac{1 - \alpha}{\alpha}\right)^{\sigma}$

    which in implicit form is the linear expansion path

    $r_2^\sigma x_2 - b r_1^\sigma x_1 = 0$

2. $q_1 = 10 - 0.2\, x_1$

    $q_2 = 20 - 1.2\, x_2$

3. (a) Convex to origin isoquants. Strictly concave for $x_1 > 0, x_2 > 0$.

    (b) Convex to origin isoquants. Concave for $x_1 > 0, x_2 > 0, x_3 > 0$.

4. Maximize $L = U(x_1, x_2) - \lambda(p_1 x_1 + p_2 x_2 - M)$

    $L_1 = U_1 - \lambda p_1 = 0$

    $L_2 = U_2 - \lambda p_2 = 0$

    $L = -p_1 x_1 - p_2 x_2 + M = 0$

Solving for λ yields

$$\lambda = \frac{U_1}{p_1} = \frac{U_2}{p_2}$$

Recall that the constraint is $M = p_1 x_1 + p_2 x_2$.

Thus $p_1 = \dfrac{\partial M}{\partial x_1}$ and $p_2 = \dfrac{\partial M}{\partial x_2}$

Thus substituting the above expressions for p_1 and p_2

then $\lambda = \dfrac{\partial U/\partial x_1}{\partial M/\partial x_1} = \dfrac{\partial U/\partial x_2}{\partial M/\partial x_2} = \dfrac{dU}{dM}$

or marginal utility of income.

5. If the first order conditions as for problem 4 are totally differentiated the following system results

$$U_{11}\,dx_1 + U_{12}\,dx_2 - \lambda\,dP_1 - P_1\,d\lambda = 0 \qquad [1]$$

$$U_{21}\,dx_1 + U_{22}\,dx_2 - \lambda\,dP_2 - P_2\,d\lambda = 0 \qquad [2]$$

$$dY - x_1\,dP_1 - P_1\,dx_1 - x_2\,dP_2 - P_2\,dx_2 = 0 \qquad [3]$$

Rearranging

$$U_{11}\,dx_1 + U_{12}\,dx_2 - P_1\,d\lambda = dP_1 \qquad [4]$$

$$U_{21}\,dx_1 + U_{22}\,dx_2 - P_2\,d\lambda = dP_2 \qquad [5]$$

$$-P_1\,dx_1 - P_2\,dx_2 = -dY + x_1\,dP_1 + x_2\,dP_2 \qquad [6]$$

Solving for dx_1 by Cramer's rule

$$dx_1 = \frac{\lambda\,dP_1 D_{11} + \lambda\,dP_2 D_{21} + (-dY + x_1\,dP_1 + x_2\,dP_2)D_{31}}{D} \qquad [7]$$

Divide both sides of [7] by dP_1 on assumption that Y and X_1 are unchanged thus

$$\frac{\partial x_1}{\partial p_1} = \frac{\lambda D_{11}}{D} + \frac{X_1 D_{31}}{D} \qquad \text{(Slutsky equation)} \qquad [8]$$

Divide [7] by dY and assuming dP_1 and dP_2 unchanged

$$\frac{\partial x_1}{\partial Y} = -\frac{D_{31}}{D} \qquad [9]$$

If in the Slutsky equation it is assumed that a given change in P_1 is accompanied by a corresponding change in income such that the consumer is neither better nor worse off than before the price change it follows that

$$dU = U_1 \, dx_1 + U_2 \, dx_2 = 0 \quad \text{or} \quad \frac{U_1}{U_2} = -\frac{dx_2}{dx_1} \tag{10}$$

From the equilibrium conditions $\dfrac{P_1}{P_2} = \dfrac{U_1}{U_2}$ [10] becomes

$$P_1 \, dx_1 + P_2 \, dx_2 = 0 \tag{11}$$

Substituting [11] into [6]

$$-dY + x_1 \, dP_1 + x_2 \, dP_2 = 0$$

From [7] $\left(\dfrac{\partial x_1}{\partial P_1}\right)_{dU=0} = \dfrac{\lambda D_{11}}{D}$ $\tag{12}$

Substitute [12] in [9]

$$\frac{\partial x_1}{\partial P_1} = \left(\frac{\partial x_1}{\partial P_1}\right)_{dU=0} - X_1 \left(\frac{\partial x_1}{\partial Y}\right)_{dP_1 = dP_2 = 0} \tag{13}$$

[13] is the final form of the Slutsky equation the first term on the right-hand side being the substitution effect and the second term being the income effect.

7.   Total cost = $2q + 3$.

For a more general procedure than that given in the text see Brems (1967).

8.   (a) $q = 4$ Check the second order conditions to confirm this shows that MC is increasing at $q = 4$. Notice that the firm actually incurs a loss at this output.
      (b) $q = 4$
      (c) AVC = 9
      (d) $q = 4$
Notice that although the firm incurs a loss it is apparently indifferent about continuing production in the short run as it is just covering variable costs.

9. $P = -\frac{11}{4} q^2$.

10.   Rank plants in ascending order of operating costs, to give a rising operating cost curve. In the long run replace high operating cost plant if the present value of the operating cost savings exceeds the capital expenditure on new plant.

Chapter 3

2. Working through the possibilities will show with the exception of (5) that they do not satisfy the K-T conditions. The rationale of this result depends on the Kuhn-Tucker theory which shows that the K-T conditions are necessary and sufficient for a global maximum when a concave function is optimized over a convex set. For a rather difficult but comprehensive treatment of these problems see Hadley (1964, pp. 84–5, 183–205).

5. $P_1 = 28, P_2 = 16$
$x_1 = 22, x_2 = 7$

Given the vector of actual quantities of $(q_{11}, \ldots, \bar{q}_2)$ it is possible to solve for optimal prices from the K-T conditions. For a complete description of the problem and solution procedure see Crew and Kleindorfer (1971).

Chapter 4

1. All firms would expand capacity simultaneously shifting the industry supply curve to the right and depressing price so that each firm had excess capacity. Further adjustment would have to take place until long run equilibrium was achieved.

2. Partially differentiate the Cobb–Douglas function $q = Ax_1^\alpha x_2^{1-\alpha}$ to obtain all four second-partial derivatives, the Hessian of which is zero. Except for a factor of proportionality with constant factor prices the Hessian of the firm's profit function is equal to the Hessian of its production function.

3.   (a)   MR = MC = 10
      (b) $x = 40$
      (c) $p = 30$
      (d)   TR = 1 200
      (e)   VC = 400
      (f)   TC = 900
      (g) $\Pi = 300$
      (h) $\eta = \frac{3}{2}$

4. (a) (i) $P = 30$, $x = 40$, $\Pi = -100$

(ii) The firm produces nothing (on the assumption that the tax is avoided if the firm ceases to produce).

(b) (i) The firm goes out of business.

5. (a) $p_1 = 35$, $p_2 = 27\frac{1}{2}$

(b) $x_1 = \dfrac{50}{3}$, $x_2 = \dfrac{70}{3}$

(c) $\eta_1 = \dfrac{7}{5}$, $\eta_2 = \dfrac{11}{7}$

(d) $\Pi_D = 1\,225 - 700 = 525$ (with price discrimination)

$\Pi = 1\,200 - 700 = 500$ (without price discrimination).

6. From equating MR and MC it is clear that $p = 30$ and $x = 40$. This is the supply relationship under monopoly with stationary demand. No supply curve analogous the supply curve in perfect competition can be derived for monopoly. If demand is allowed to shift in monopoly a locus of points is traced out. However, if another set of shifts is allowed then another locus is traced out implying a non-unique relationship between price and quantity supplied. Hence the meaning of supply is not clear under monopoly. (In the diagram notice how MR_1 and MR_2 cut MC at q_2 but yield different price relationships P_1 and P_2. Thus (diagram omitted) two "supply curves" are traced out.)

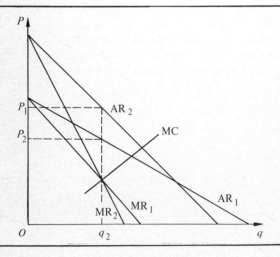

7. Solving simultaneously the following for y and z

$$y + x + a + b = L \qquad\qquad\qquad\qquad [*]$$

$$P_A + cy = P_B + cz \qquad\qquad\qquad\qquad [**]$$

$$y = \tfrac{1}{2}\left(L - a - b + \frac{P_B - P_A}{c} \right)$$

$$z = \tfrac{1}{2}\left(L - a - b + \frac{P_A - P_B}{c} \right)$$

Profits are

$$\Pi_A = P_A(a + y) = \tfrac{1}{2}(L + a - b)P_A - \frac{P_A^2}{2c} + \frac{P_A P_B}{2c}$$

$$\Pi_B = P_B(b + z) = \tfrac{1}{2}(L - a + b)P_B - \frac{P_B^2}{2c} + \frac{P_A P_B}{2c}$$

Taking partial derivatives of Π_A and Π_B respectively, with respect to P_A and P_B, and solving simultaneously yields

$$P_A = c\left(L + \frac{a - b}{3} \right)$$

$$P_B = c\left(L - \frac{a - b}{3} \right)$$

8. B initially sells $Q_1 Q_2 = Q_2 Q$. He increases his output to $\tfrac{1}{2}(OQ - \tfrac{1}{2}OQ) = \tfrac{1}{2}(OQ - \tfrac{3}{8}OQ = OQ(\tfrac{1}{2} - \tfrac{3}{10}) = \tfrac{5}{16}$. He thus expands $\tfrac{5}{16} - \tfrac{1}{4} = \tfrac{1}{16}$. His next expansion will be $\tfrac{1}{64}$, his next $\tfrac{1}{256}$, $\tfrac{1}{1024}$, and so on. The sum of these is $\tfrac{1}{4} + \tfrac{1}{16} + \tfrac{1}{64} + \tfrac{1}{256} + \tfrac{1}{1024} + \ldots$ converges at $\tfrac{1}{3}$.

Chapter 5

1. Writing in matrix form yields

$$\begin{bmatrix} \dfrac{\partial^2 U}{\partial z_1^2} & \dfrac{\partial^2 U}{\partial z_1 \partial z_2} \\[2ex] \dfrac{\partial^2 U}{\partial z_2 \partial z_1} & \dfrac{\partial^2 U}{\partial z_2^2} \end{bmatrix} \begin{bmatrix} \dfrac{\partial z_1}{\partial \alpha_1} & \dfrac{\partial z_1}{\partial \alpha_2} & \dfrac{\partial z_1}{\partial \alpha_3} \\[2ex] \dfrac{\partial z_2}{\partial \alpha_1} & \dfrac{\partial z_2}{\partial \alpha_2} & \dfrac{\partial z_2}{\partial \alpha_3} \end{bmatrix}$$

$$+ \begin{bmatrix} \dfrac{\partial^2 U}{\partial z_1 \, \partial \alpha_2} & \dfrac{\partial^2 U}{\partial z_1 \, \partial \alpha_2} & \dfrac{\partial^2 U}{\partial z_1 \, \partial \alpha_3} \\[2em] \dfrac{\partial^2 U}{\partial z_2 \, \partial \alpha_1} & \dfrac{\partial^2 U}{\partial z_2 \, \partial \alpha_2} & \dfrac{\partial^2 U}{\partial z_2 \, \partial \alpha_3} \end{bmatrix} = 0$$

Solving for $\dfrac{\partial z_1}{\partial \alpha_2}$ using Cramer's rule gives

$$\frac{\partial z_1}{\partial \alpha_2} = \frac{\begin{vmatrix} -\dfrac{\partial^2 U}{\partial z_1 \, \partial \alpha_2} & \dfrac{\partial^2 U}{\partial z_1 \, \partial z_2} \\[2em] -\dfrac{\partial^2 U}{\partial z_2 \, \partial \alpha_2} & \dfrac{\partial^2 U}{\partial z_2^2} \end{vmatrix}}{\text{Det } U_{22}}$$

Where Det U_{22} denotes determinant of second partials of the utility function, i.e., the determinant of the first matrix given above. Putting in the signs from the information given in the matrix in the exercise and recalling that Det U_{22} is positive yields $\dfrac{\partial z_1}{\partial \alpha_2} = +$? and similarly for the other

sign relationships.

2.   See Appendix.

3.   It is necessary to set up a Lagrangian and to show that the Lagrange multiplier, λ is positive, because this implies a binding constraint. Thus the problem is maximizing L

$$L = R - \lambda(R - VC - WA - K).$$

This involves obtaining Kuhn-Tucker conditions as follows:

(1) $\dfrac{\partial L}{\partial A} = R_A - \lambda(R_A - W) \leqslant 0; \quad A[R_A - \lambda(R_A - W)] = 0; \quad A \geqslant 0$

(2) $\dfrac{\partial L}{\partial x} = R_x - \lambda(R_x - VC_x) \leqslant 0; \quad x[R_x - \lambda(R_x - VC_x)] = 0; \quad x \geqslant 0$

(3) $\quad \dfrac{\partial L}{\partial \lambda} = -(R - VC - WA - K) \geqslant 0; \quad -\lambda[R - VC - WA - K] = 0;$

$\quad \lambda \geqslant 0.$

Assume that the constraint is not binding. It thus follows from (3) that $\lambda = 0$. Thus for (1) and (2) $R_A \leqslant 0$, and $R_x \leqslant 0$. This contradicts the assumption that $R_A > 0$. Hence $\lambda > 0$ is proved by contradiction.

Chapter 6

1. $\quad \Pi_t = (1 - t)[(p - v)q^* - F] - \alpha(1 - t)^2(p - v)^2\sigma_u^2$

Taking the derivative with respect to $(-p)$ yields

$$\frac{\partial \hat{\Pi}_t}{\partial(-p)} = (1 - t)\,\frac{\partial \Pi^*}{\partial(-p)} - 2\alpha(1 - t)^2(p - v)\sigma_u^2 = 0 \qquad [\dagger]$$

As $(1 - t) < 1$, it follows from [6.32] and [†] that the risk aversion displayed in [†] is less than in [6.32].

2. First find

$$\frac{\mathrm{d}g_F}{\mathrm{d}i} = \frac{Am - T'(g_F)}{(i - g_F)T''(g_F)}$$

as $A = \dfrac{T(g) + (i - g)T'(g)}{a + m(f + i)}$

$$\frac{\mathrm{d}g_M}{\mathrm{d}i} = \frac{Am}{T'(g_M)} \qquad \text{when } \bar{v} = 1 \qquad\qquad [*]$$

Noting from [*] that $Am = \dfrac{\mathrm{d}g_M}{\mathrm{d}i} \cdot T'(g_M)$ it follows that (using the form $T(g) = 1 - S(g - g_m)^2$)

$$\frac{\mathrm{d}g_F}{\mathrm{d}i} = \frac{\mathrm{d}g_M/\mathrm{d}i(-2S)(g_M - g_m) - (-2S)(g_F - g_m)}{(i - g_F)(-2S)}$$

Cancelling $(-2S)$ and rearranging

$$= \frac{\mathrm{d}g_M}{\mathrm{d}i}\frac{g_M - g_m}{i - g_F} - \frac{g_F - g_m}{i - g_F}$$

This implies that $\dfrac{\mathrm{d}g_F}{\mathrm{d}i} < \dfrac{\mathrm{d}g_M}{\mathrm{d}i}$ and hence that Marris Ltd responds more to changes in i than Fisher Ltd the closer is g_F to g_M.

Index